INSTANT WALL ART:

BEAUTIFUL BOTANICAL PRINTS

READY-TO-FRAME VINTAGE ILLUSTRATIONS

ADAMS MEDIA

NEW YORK AMSTERDAM/ANTWERP LONDON TORONTO SYDNEY/MELBOURNE NEW DELHI

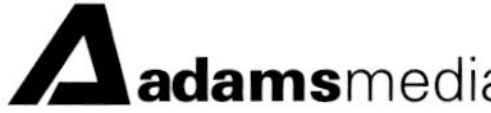

Adams Media
An Imprint of Simon & Schuster, LLC
100 Technology Center Drive
Stoughton, MA 02072

First Adams Media trade paperback edition October 2025

Interior design by Erin Alexander
Interior illustrations © Getty Images; 123RF; Lunagirl Images

Manufactured in China

10 9 8 7 6 5 4 3 2 1

ISBN 978-1-5072-2459-5

INTRODUCTION

Today, beautiful botanical prints are everywhere you look—from social media to popular design magazines and showrooms to the walls of your friends' living rooms and kitchens. And now, instead of having to choose between one or two expensive prints, you can choose from forty-five stunning illustrations found within the pages of *Instant Wall Art: Beautiful Botanical Prints* to personalize your own walls!

Extraordinarily popular in the eighteenth and nineteenth centuries, these types of prints were first drawn and hand-colored by botanists who used lovely shades of watercolor to capture the scientific details of the flora they studied. Now, with images capturing everything from the delicate blooms of the yarrow to the elegant flowers of the dogwood, you're sure to find something in this book that speaks to your design aesthetic. These nature prints measure 8" × 10" and will fit in a standard mat and frame once removed from the book at the perforated edge. So choose the prints you love, hang them on your walls, and enjoy the beauty of nature in your own home throughout the year!

THE PRINTS

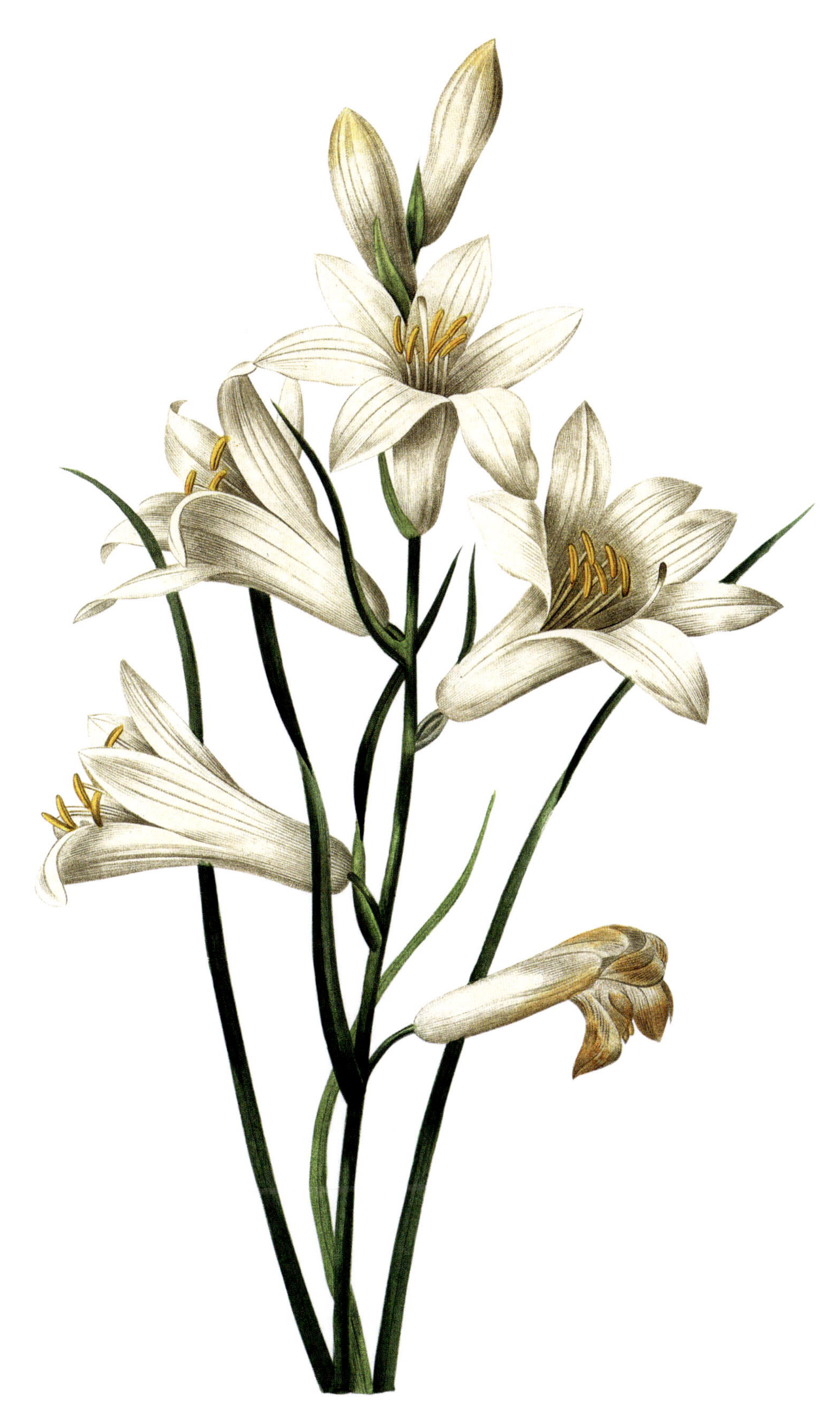

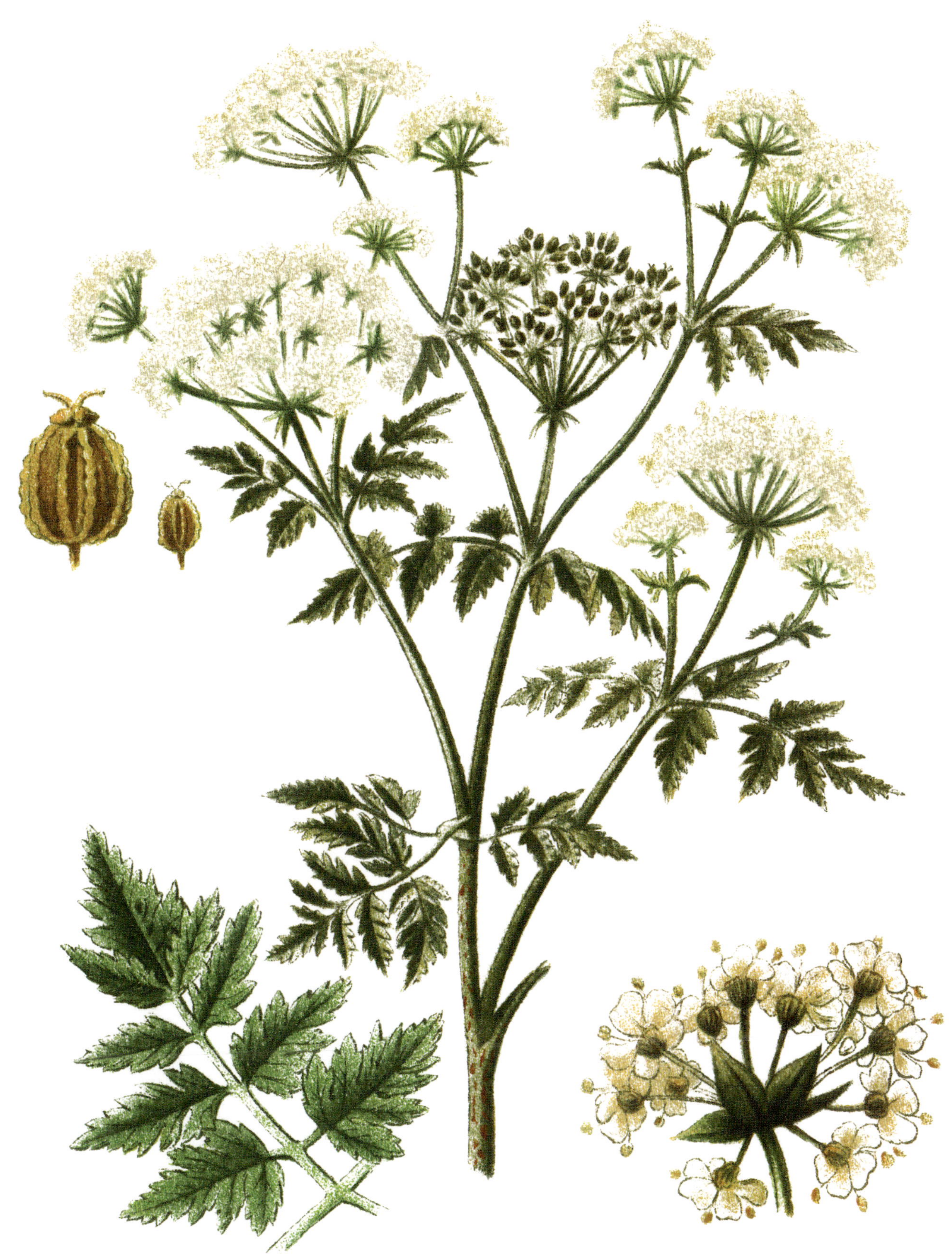

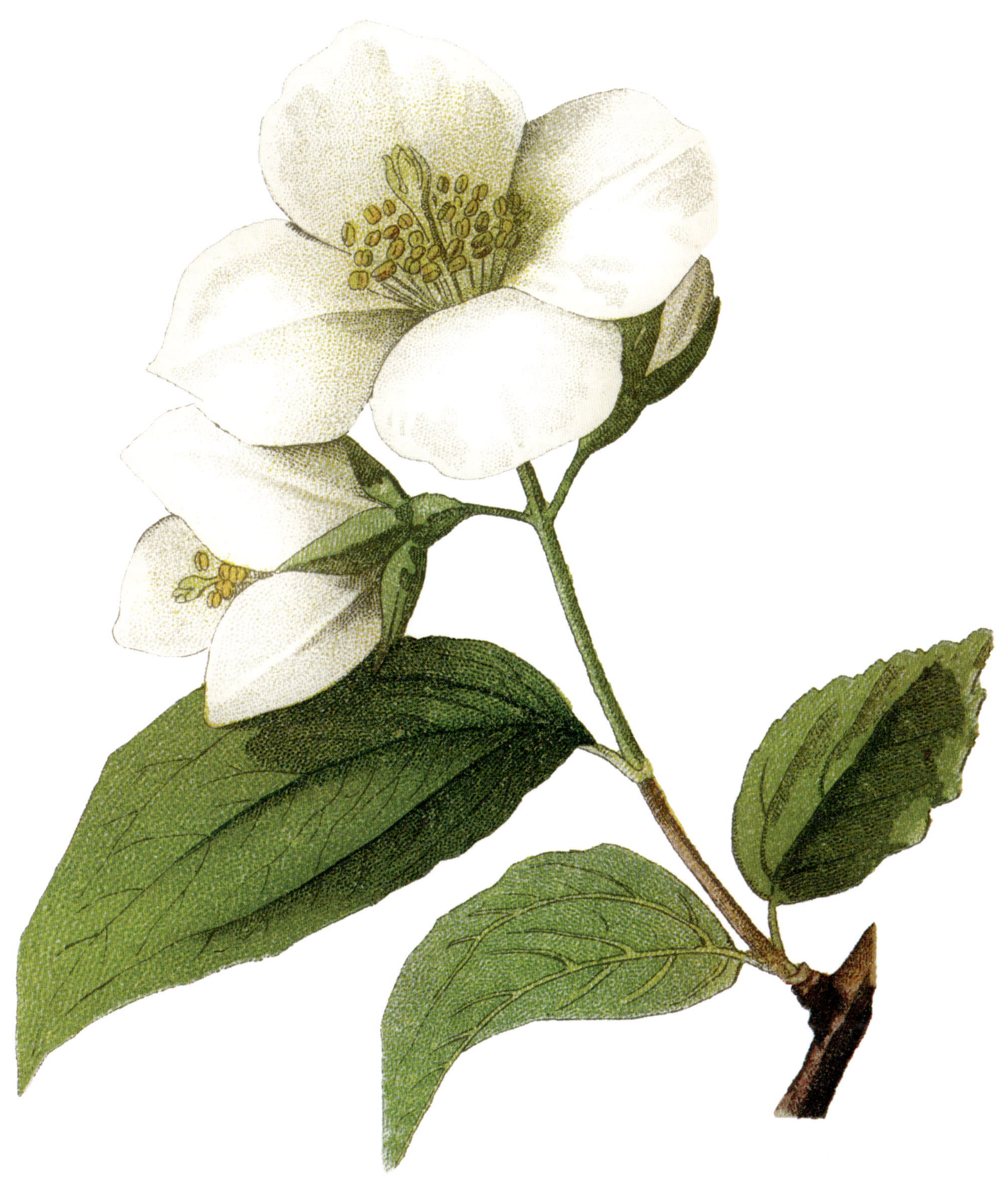

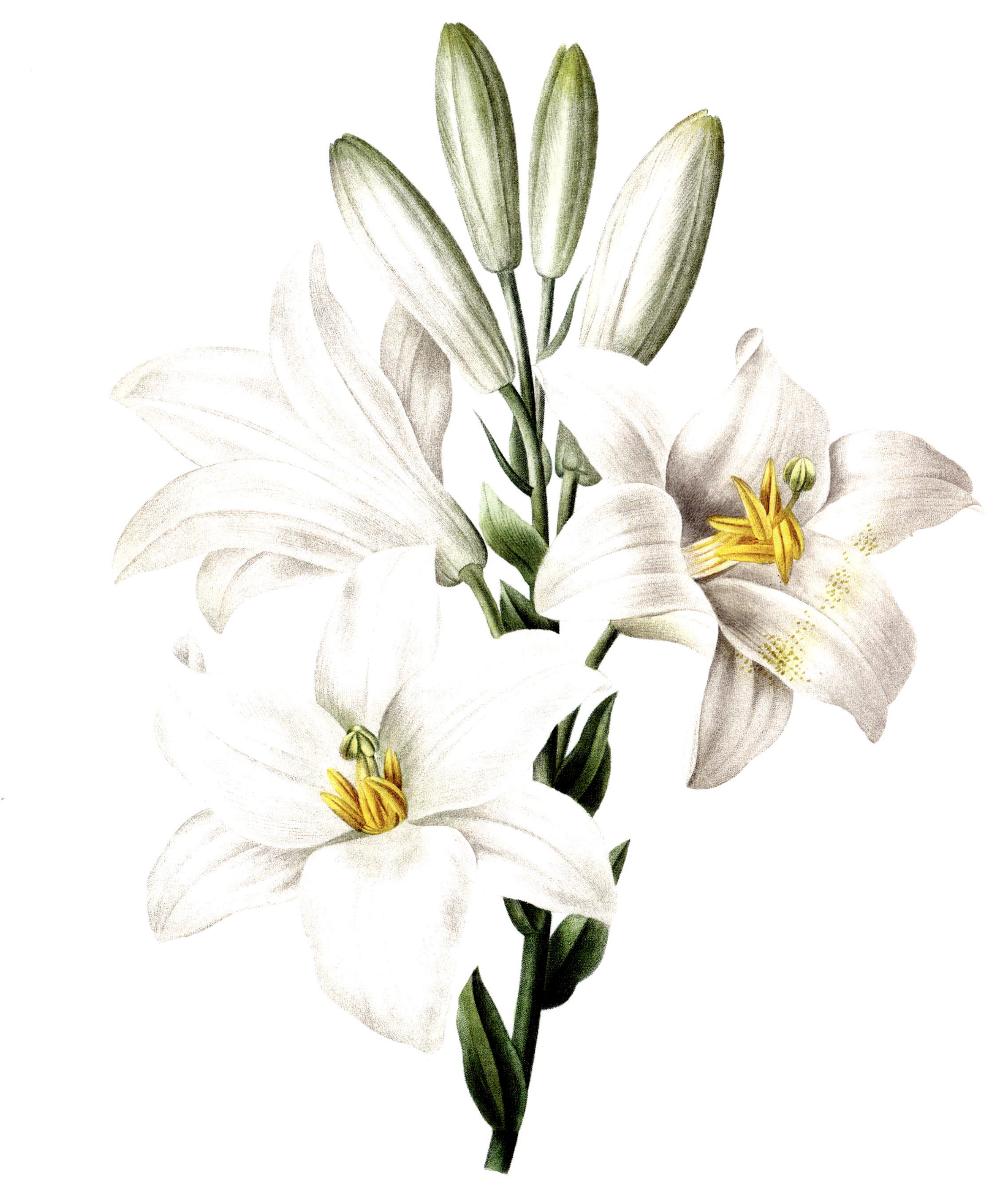

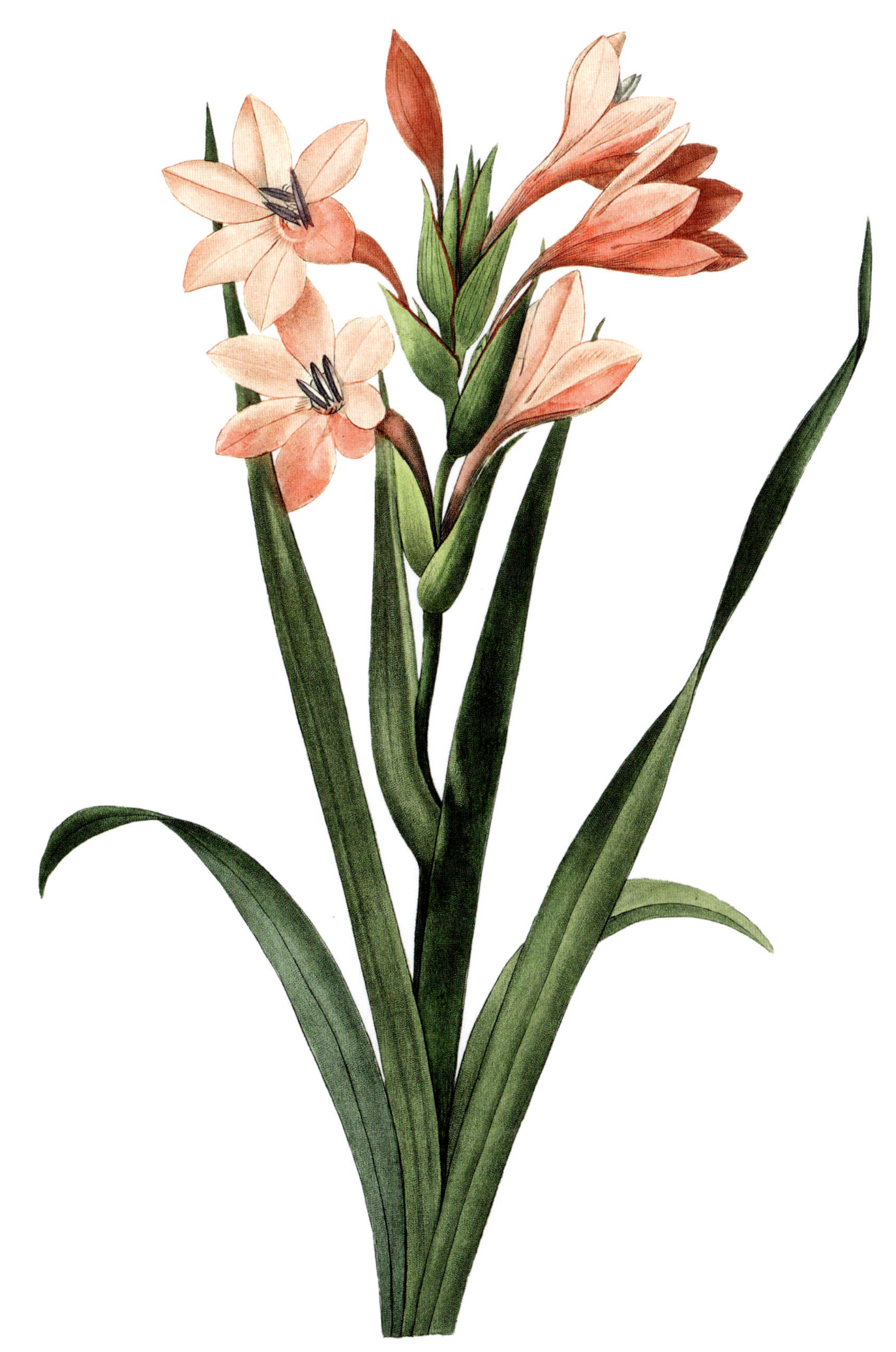

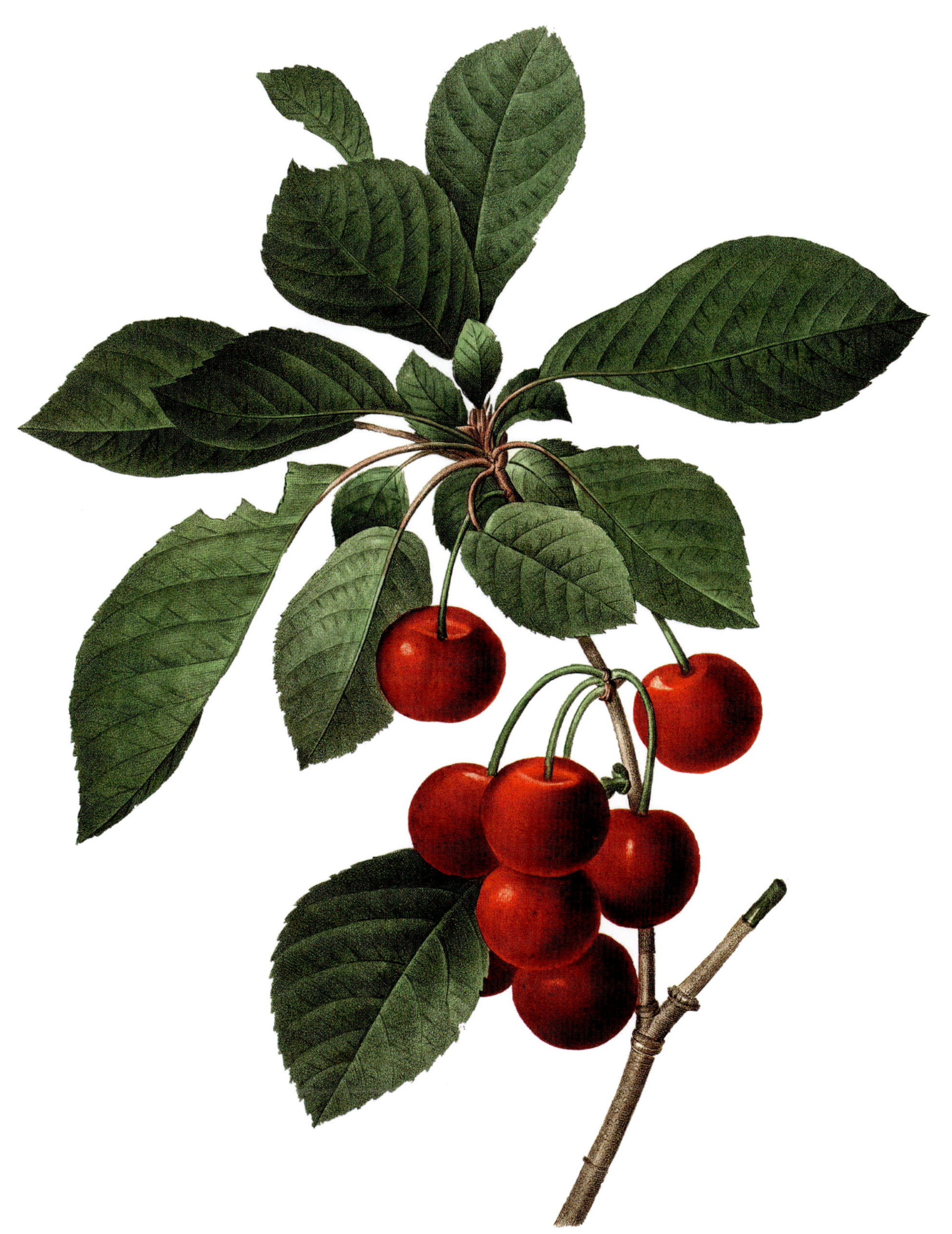

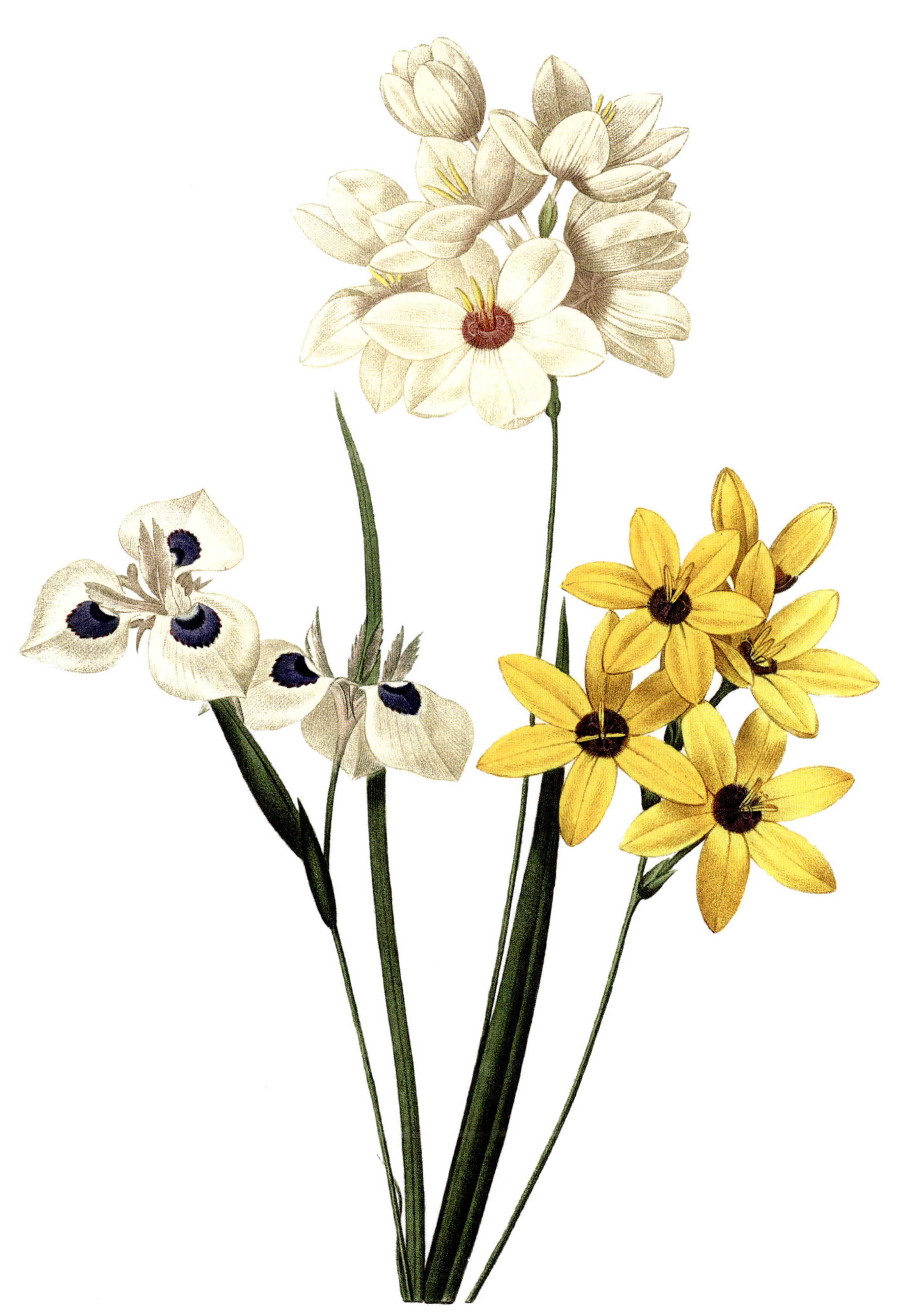

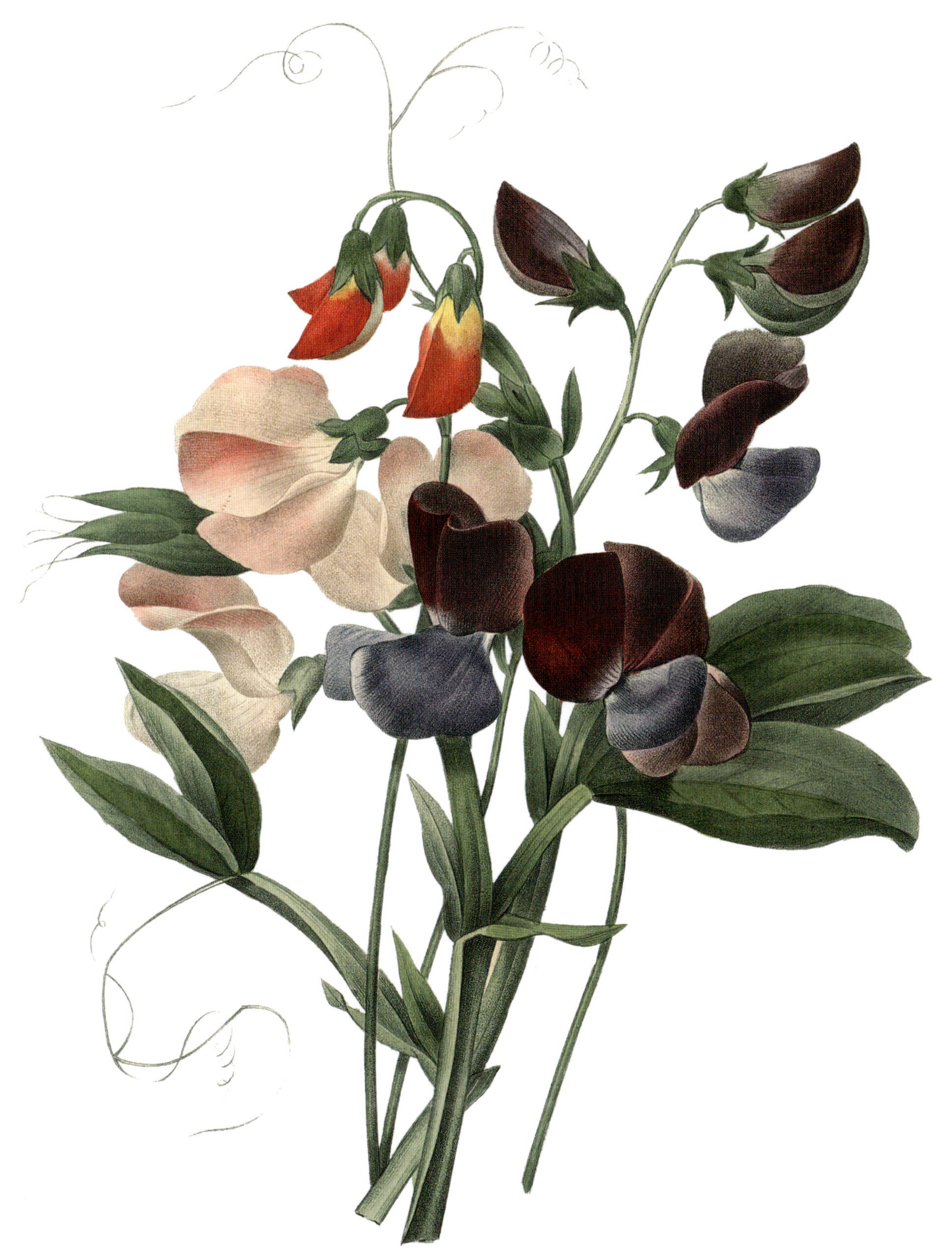

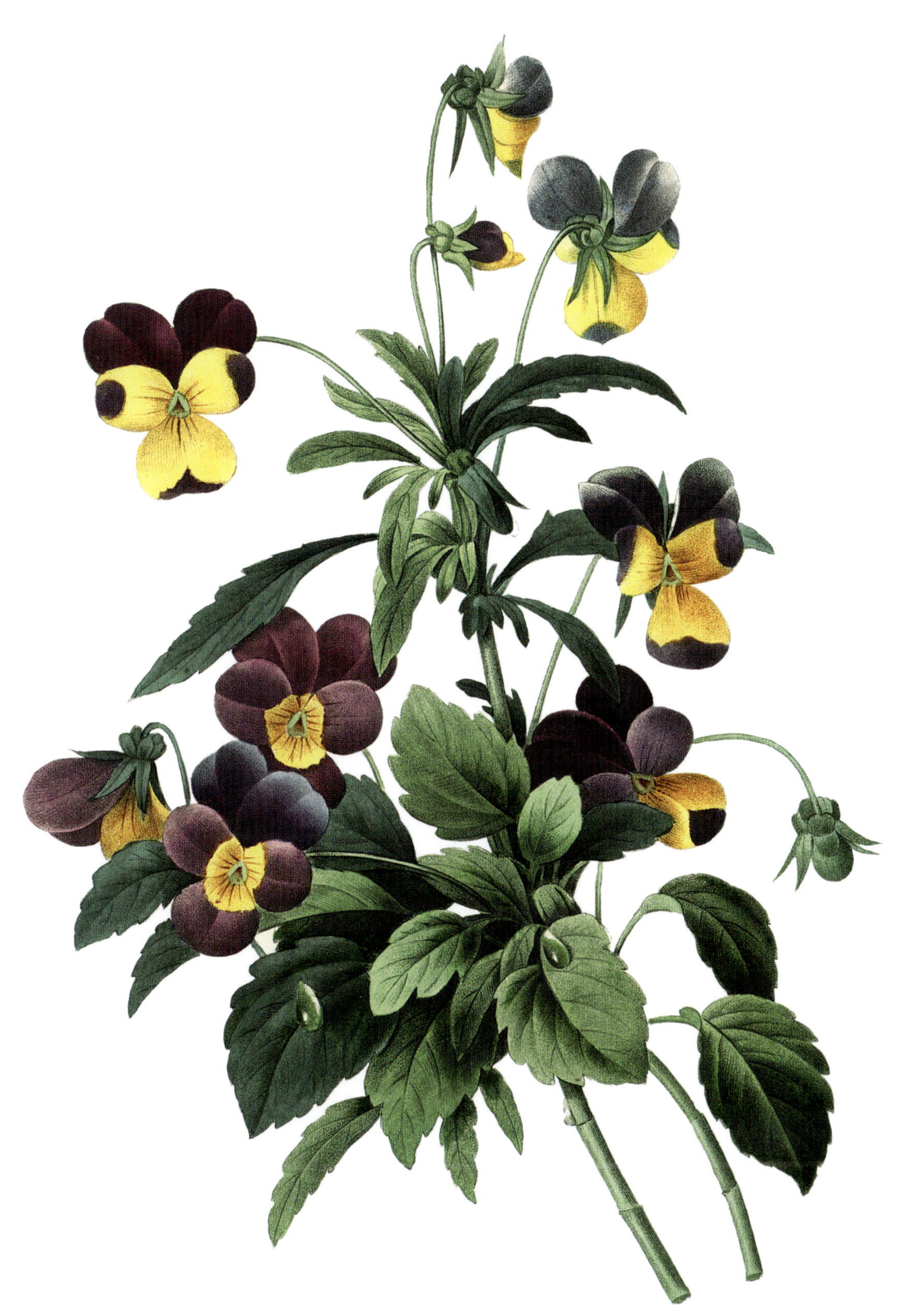

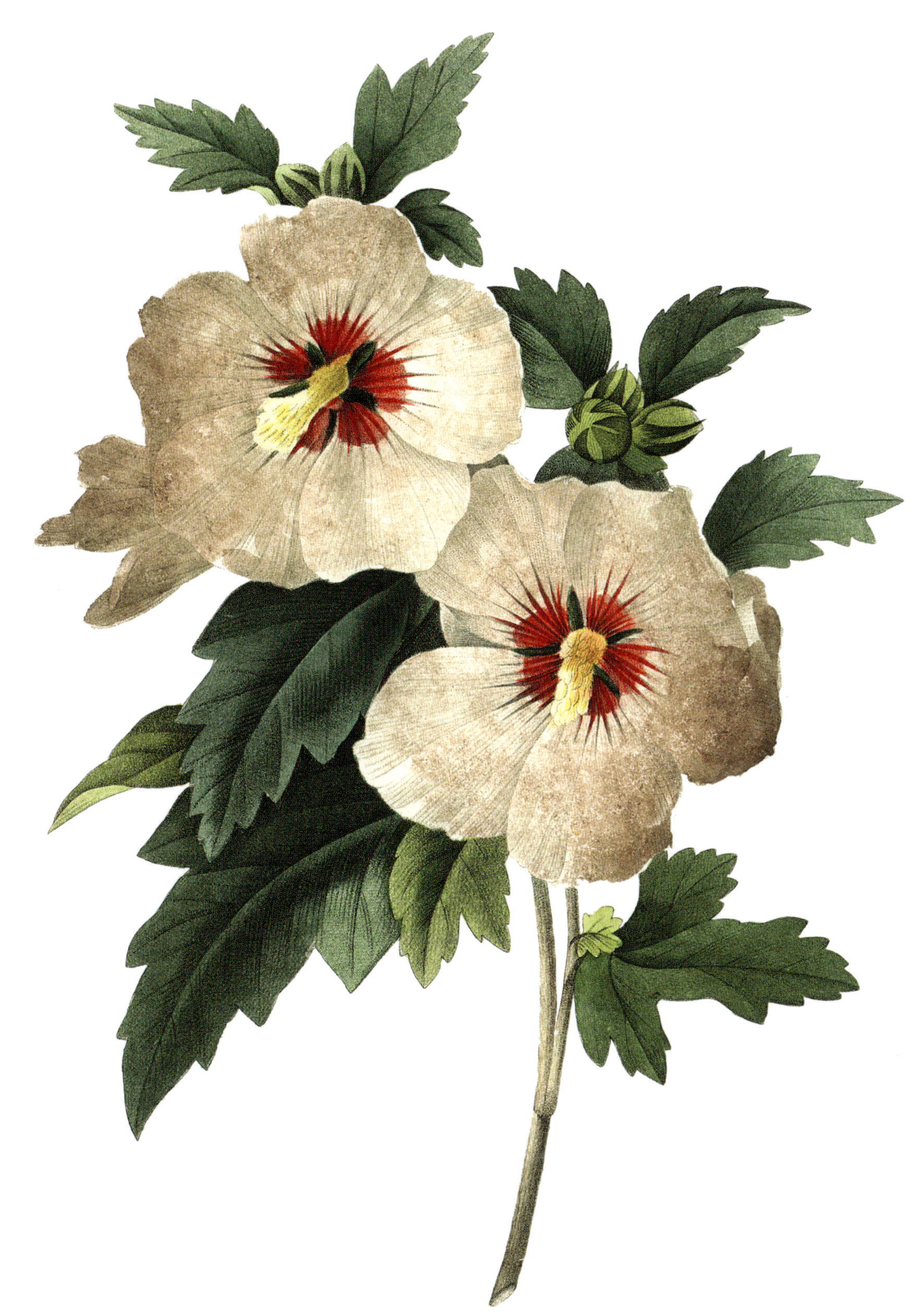

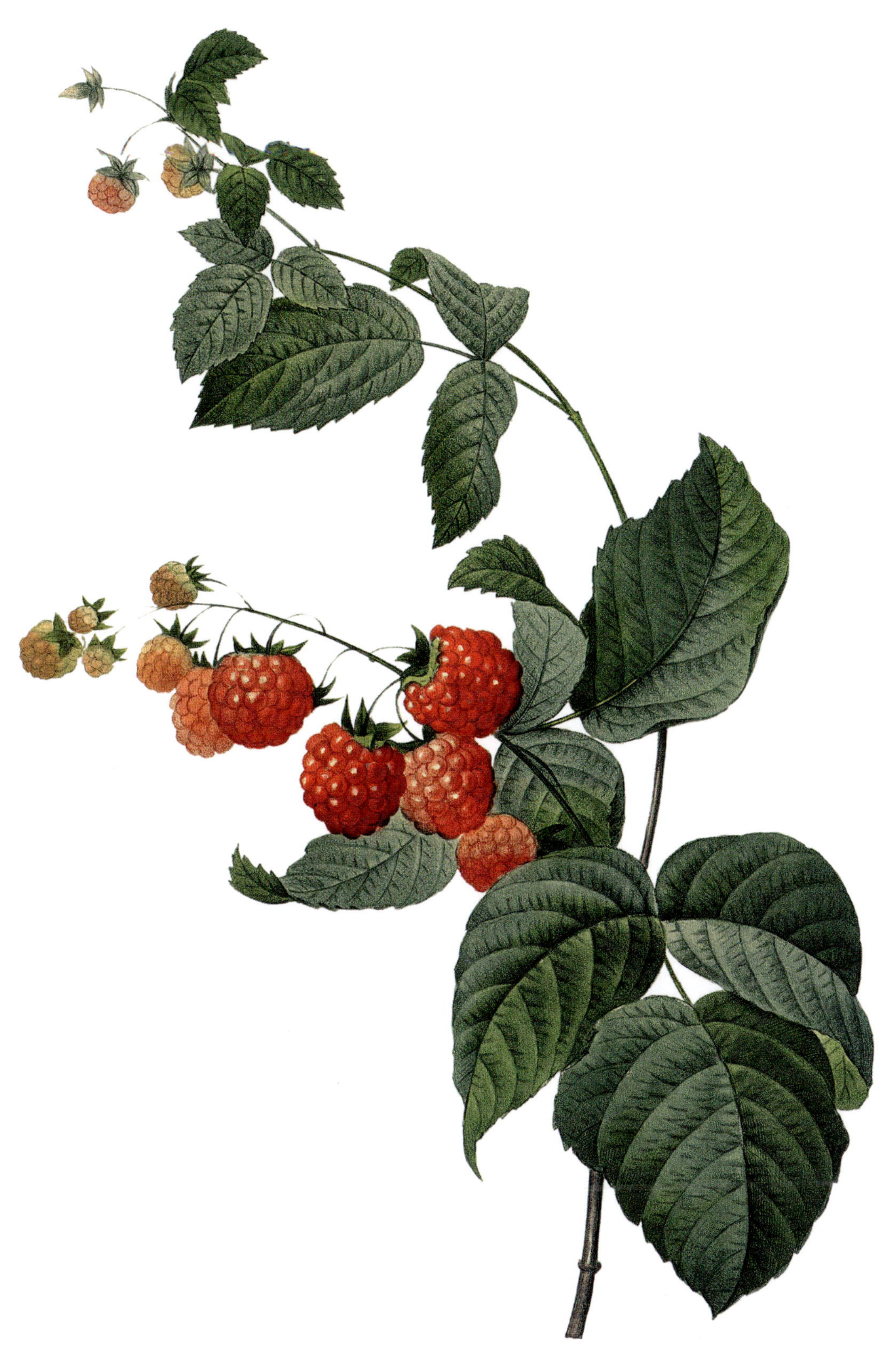

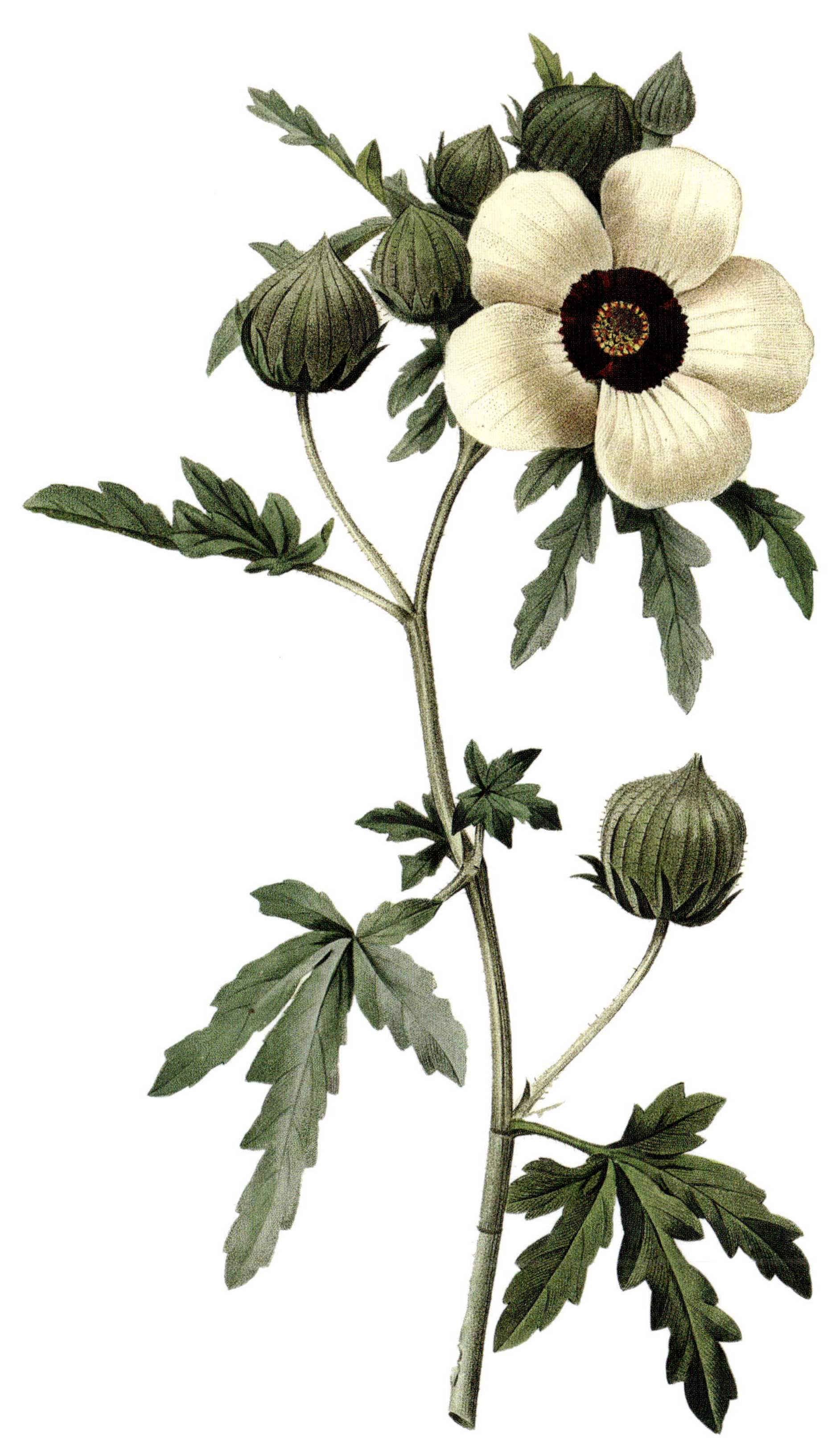

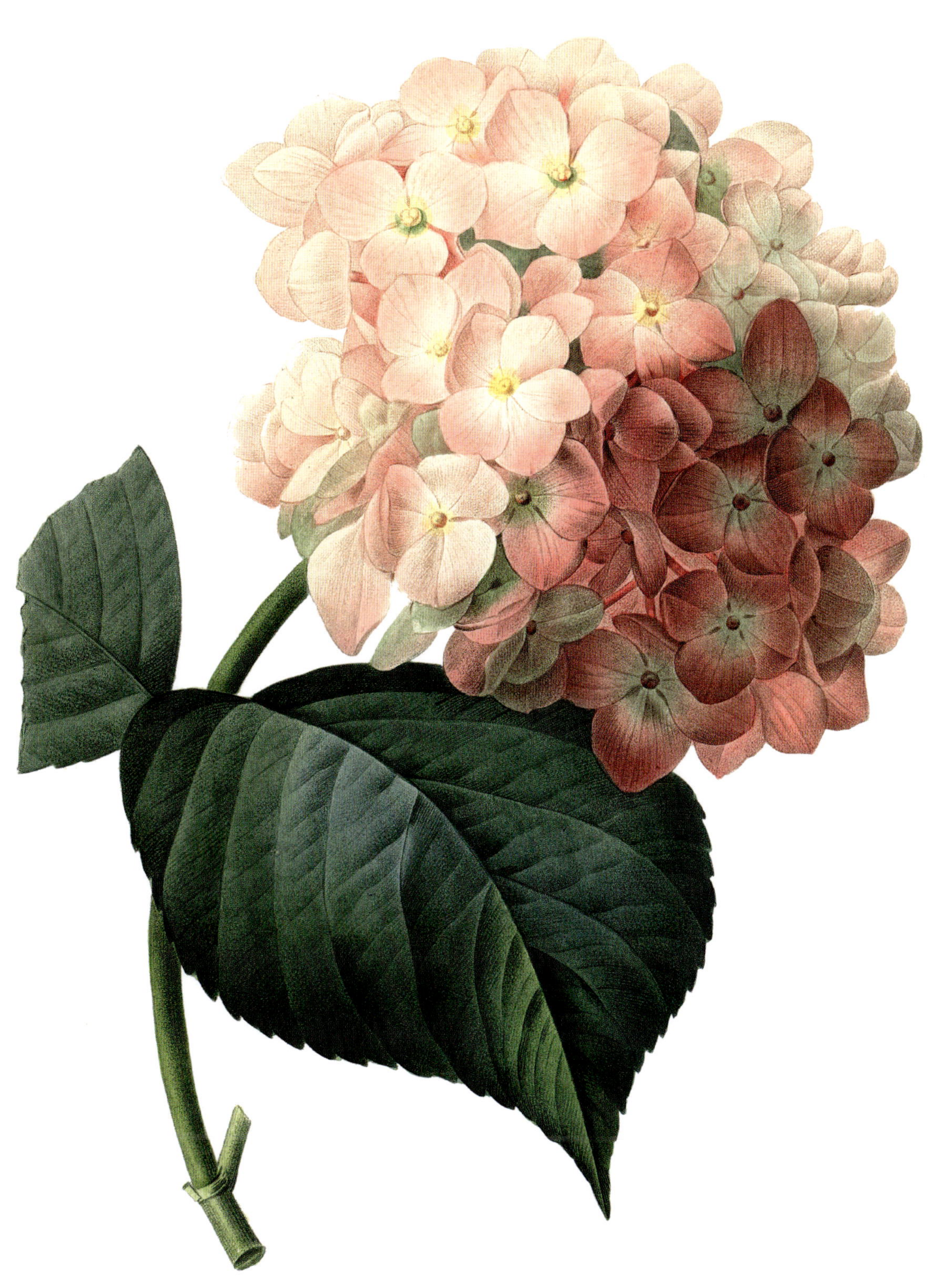

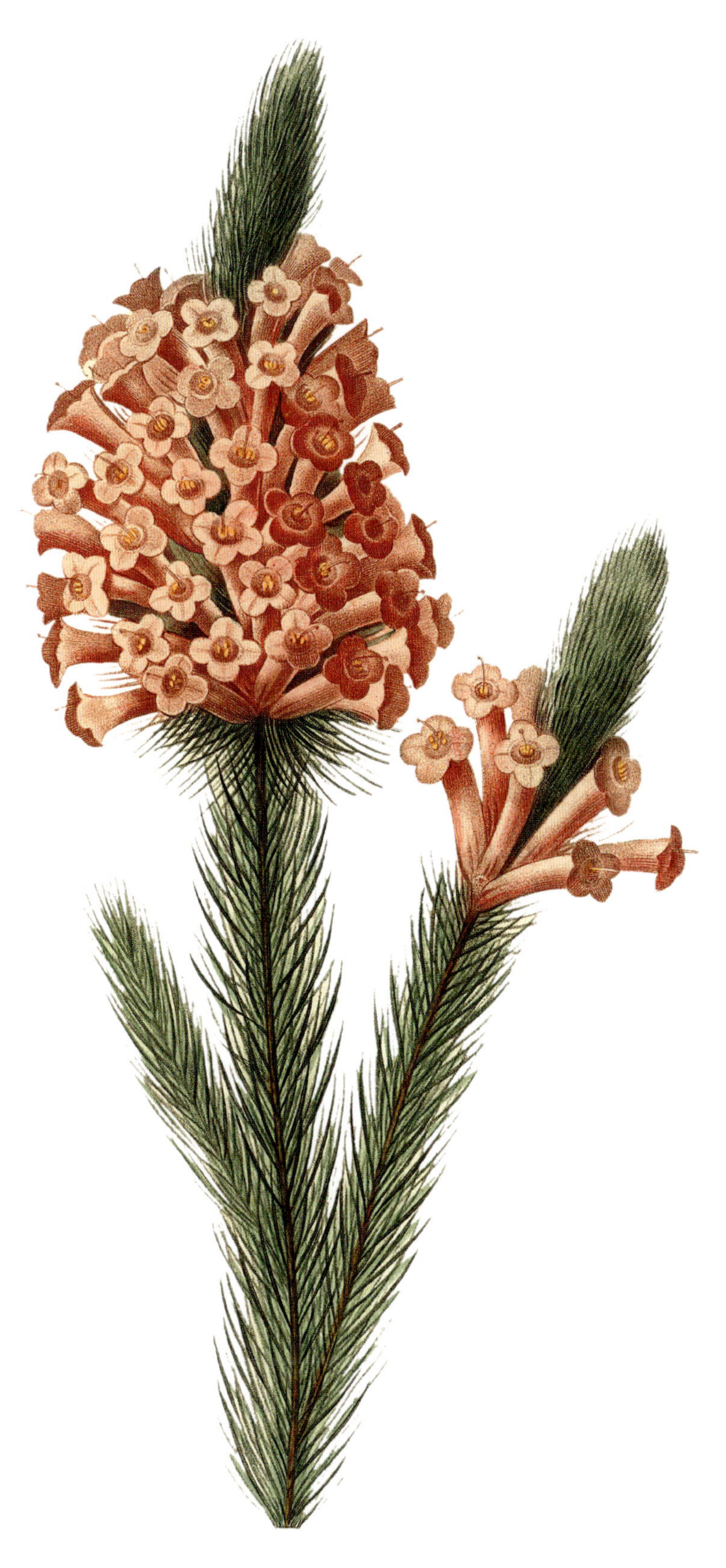

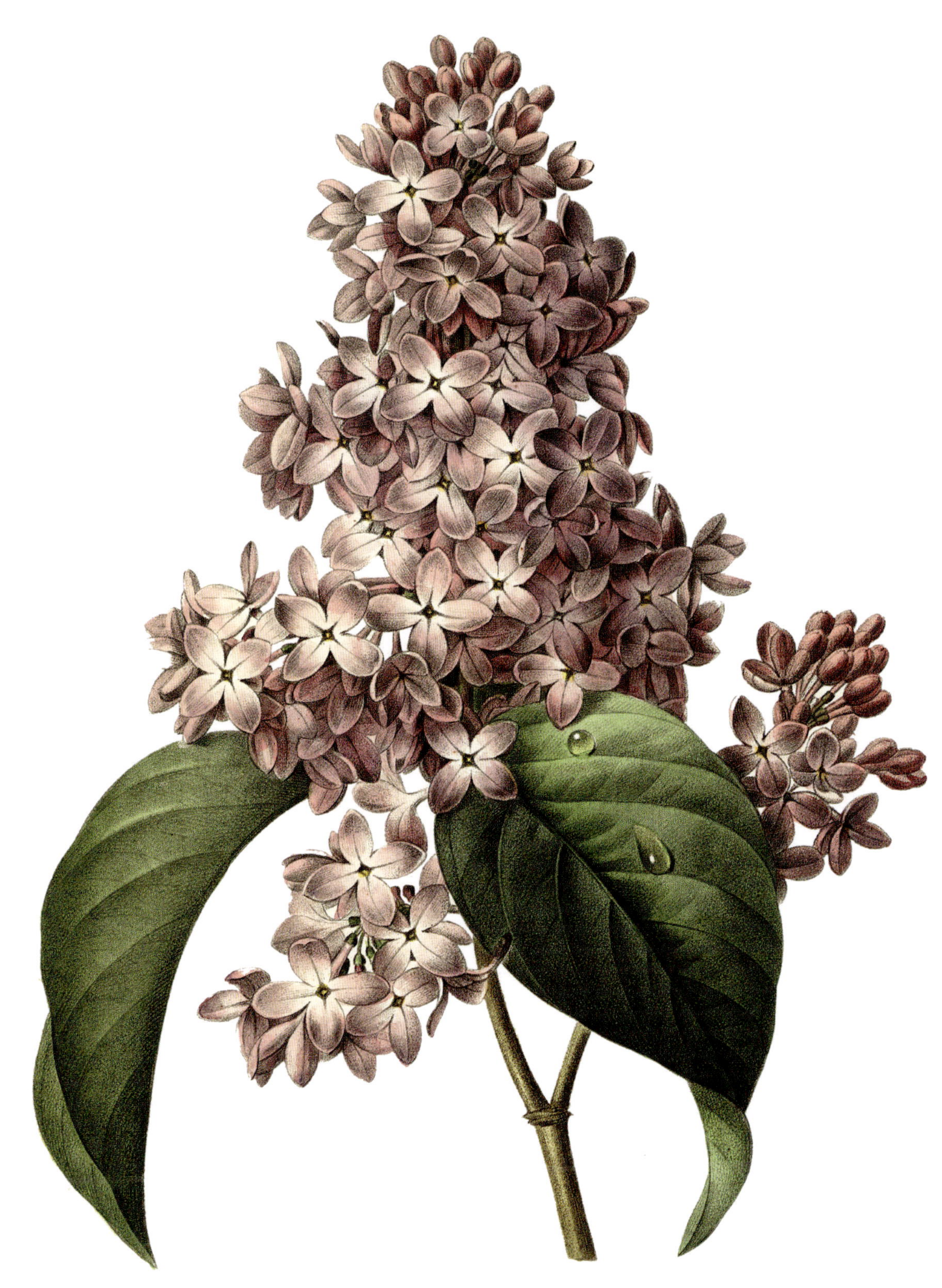

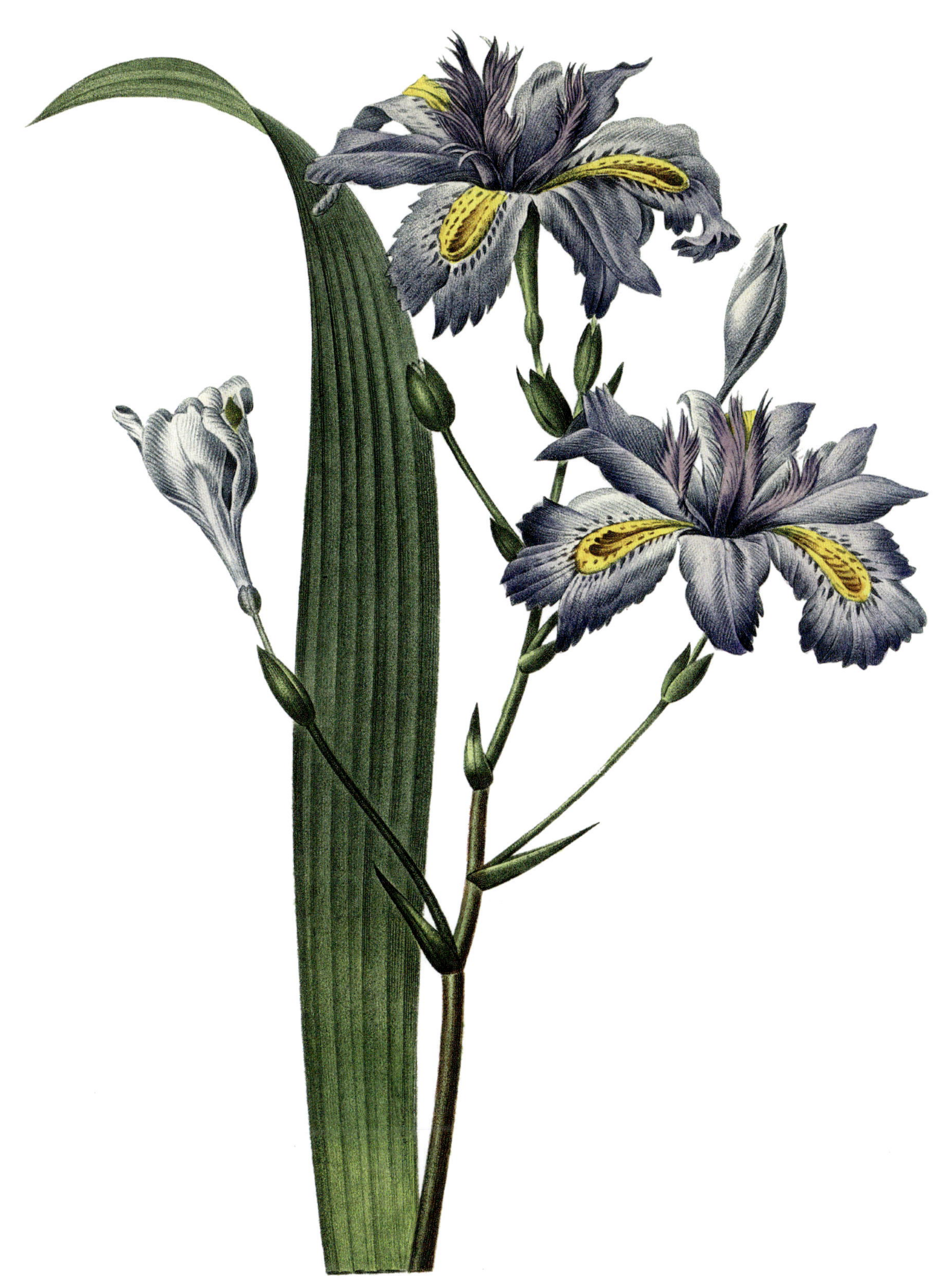

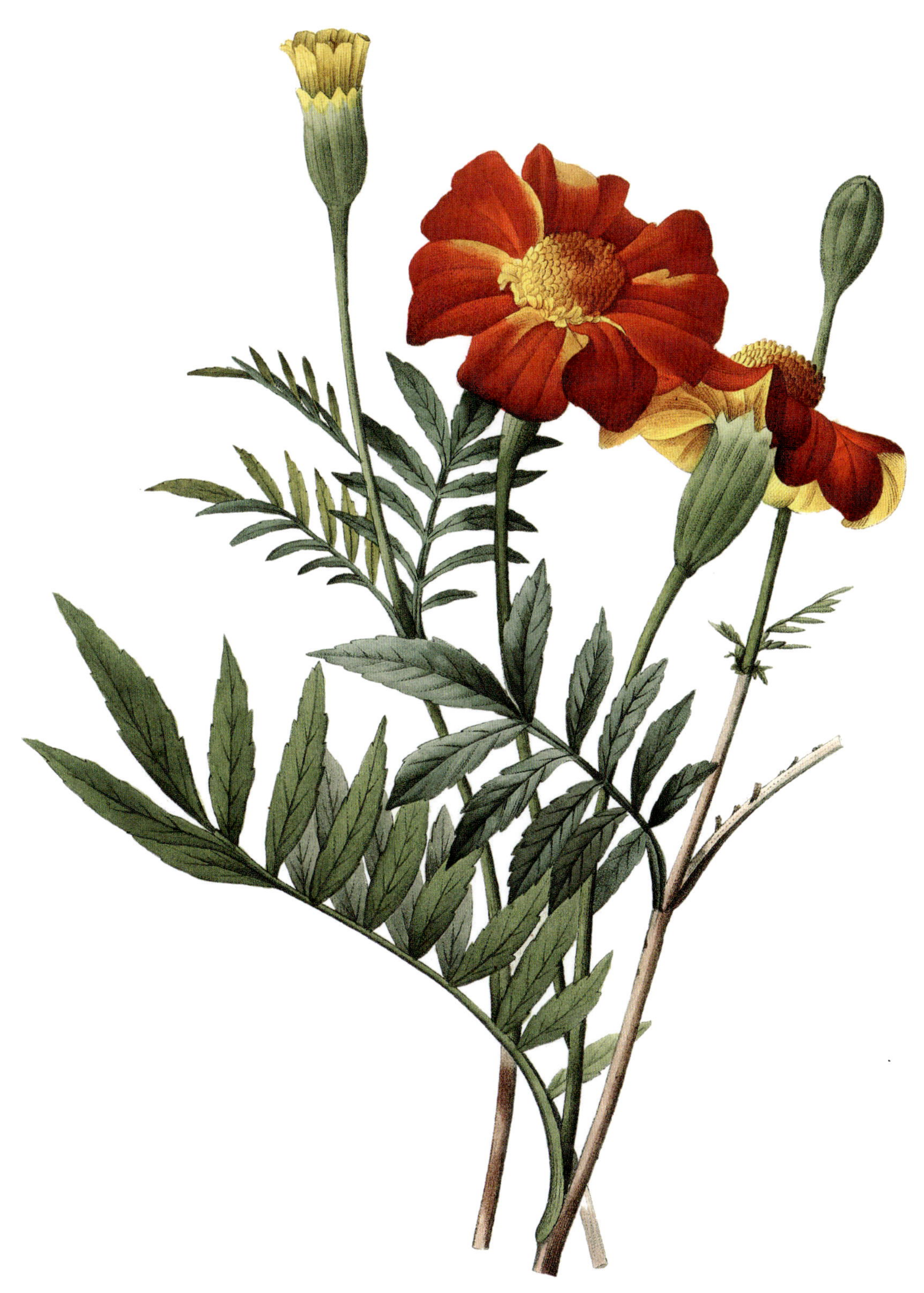

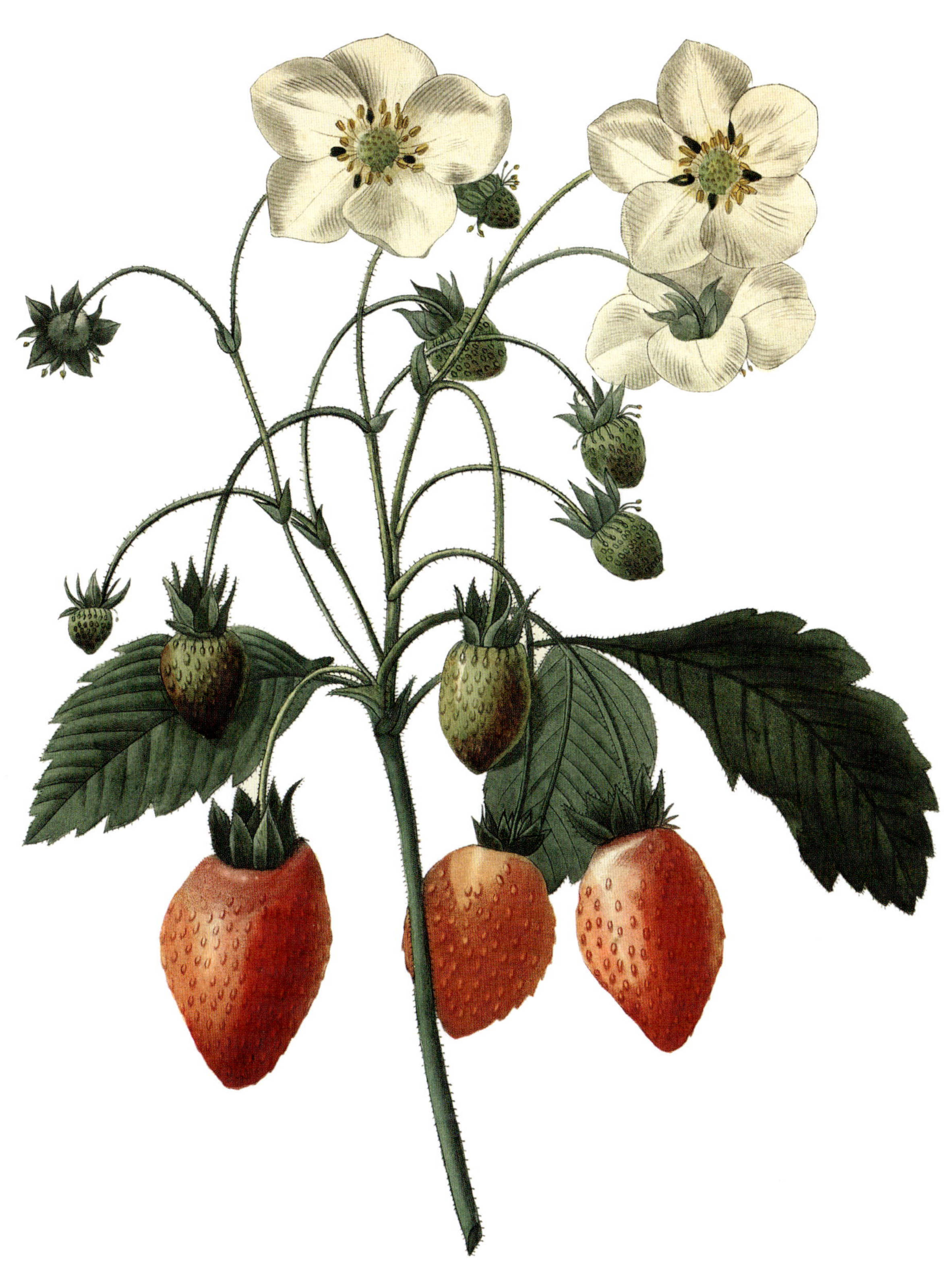

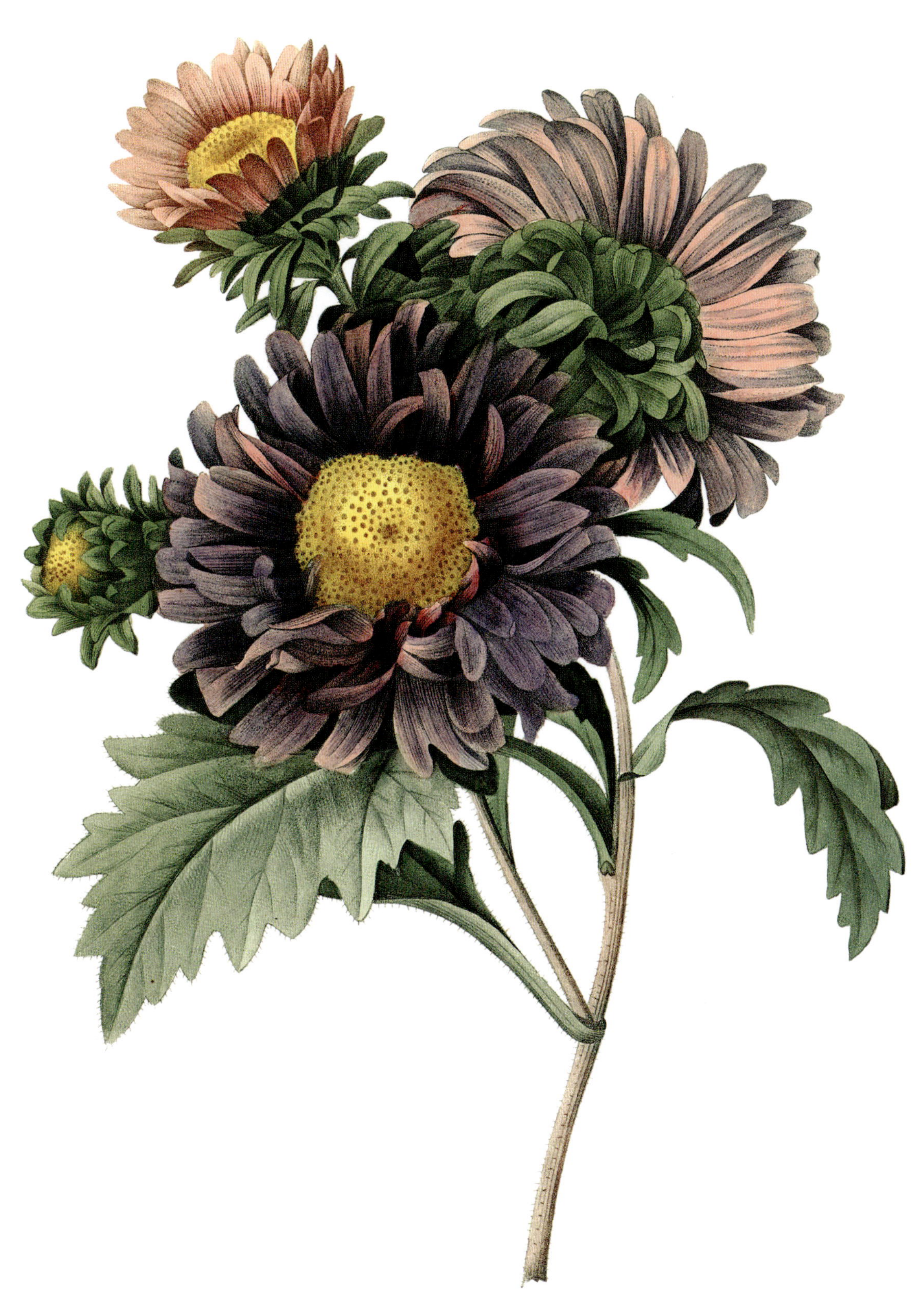

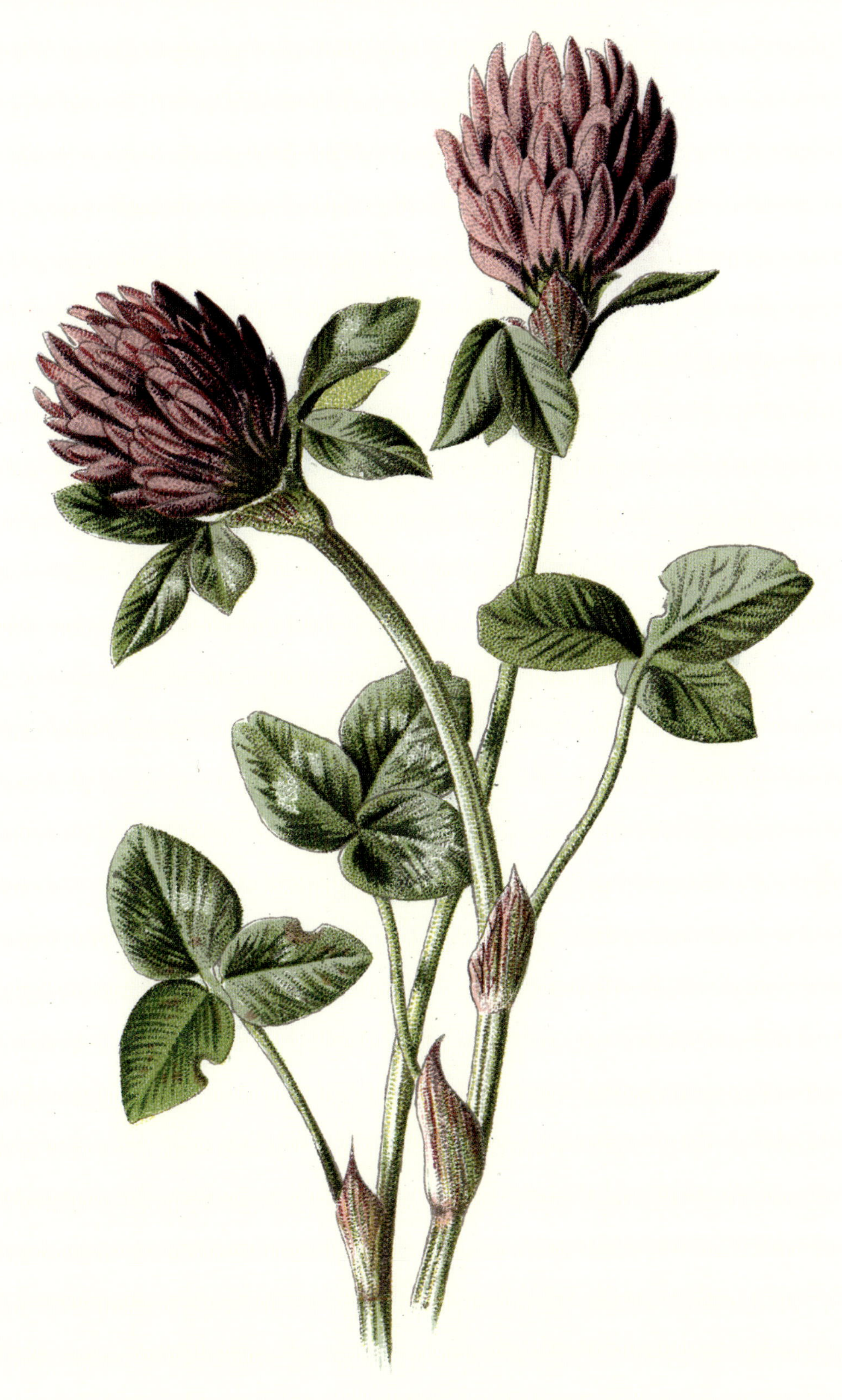

RED MEADOW-CLOVER

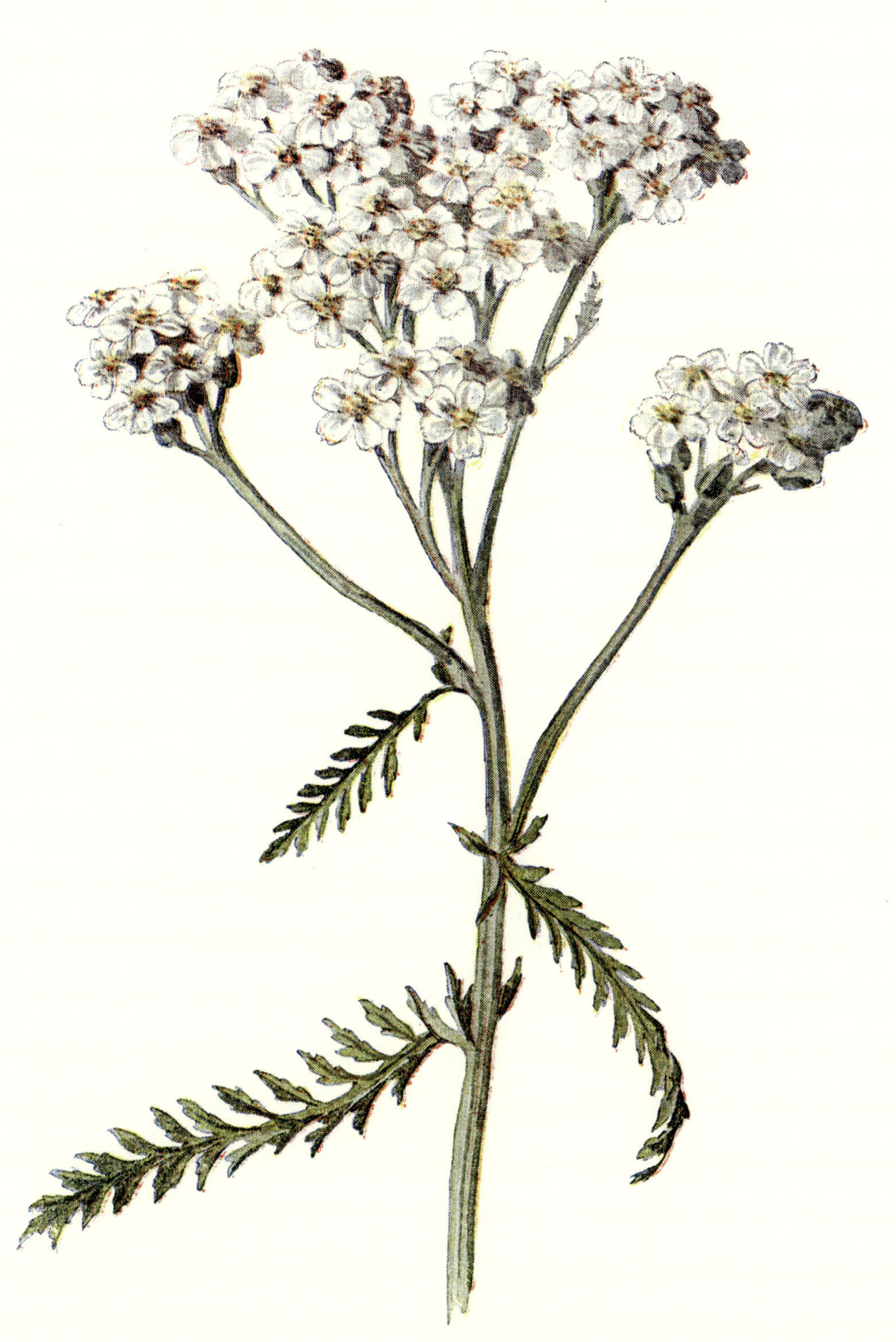

YARROW.

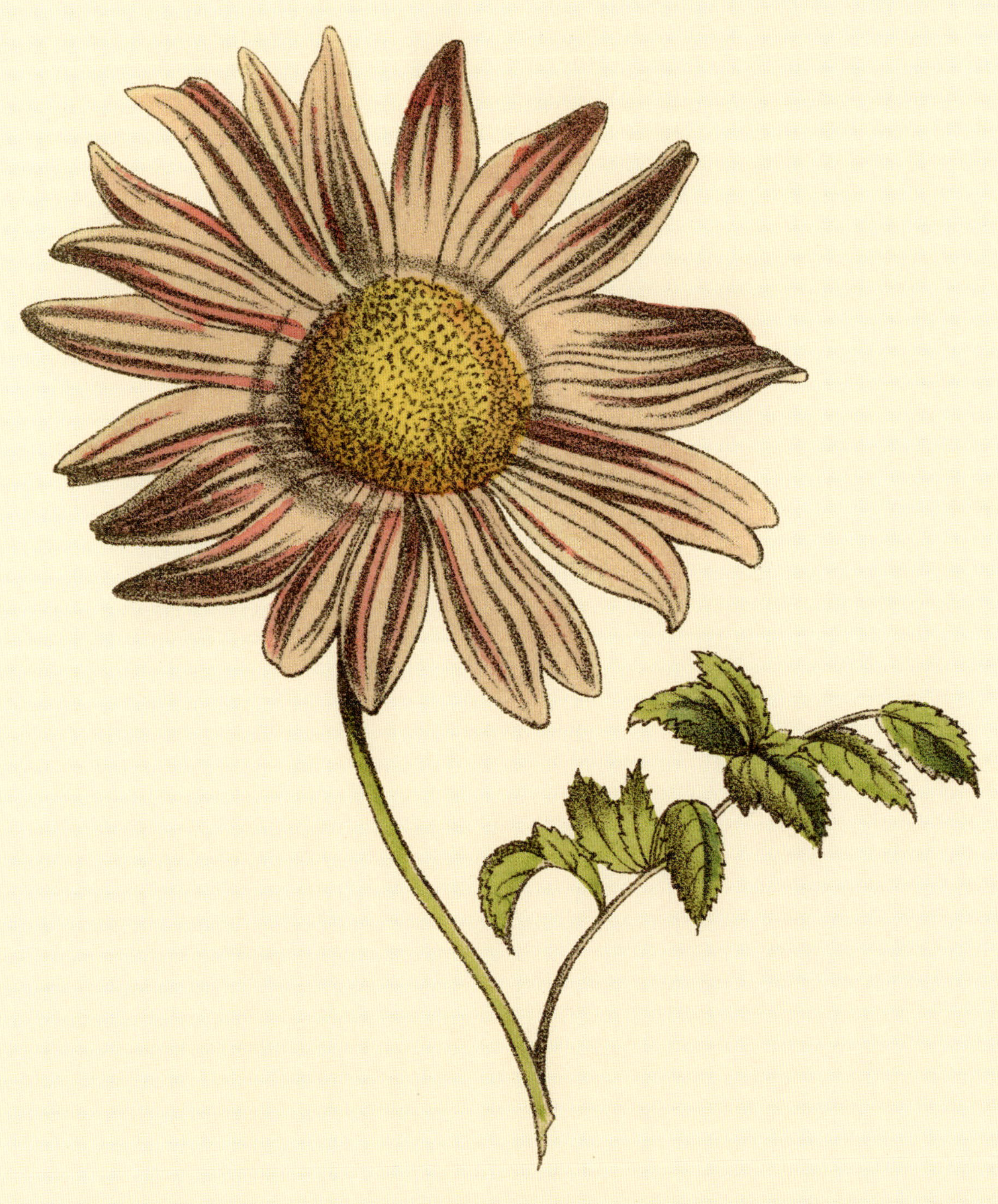

Pyrethrum
CHRYSANTHEMUM

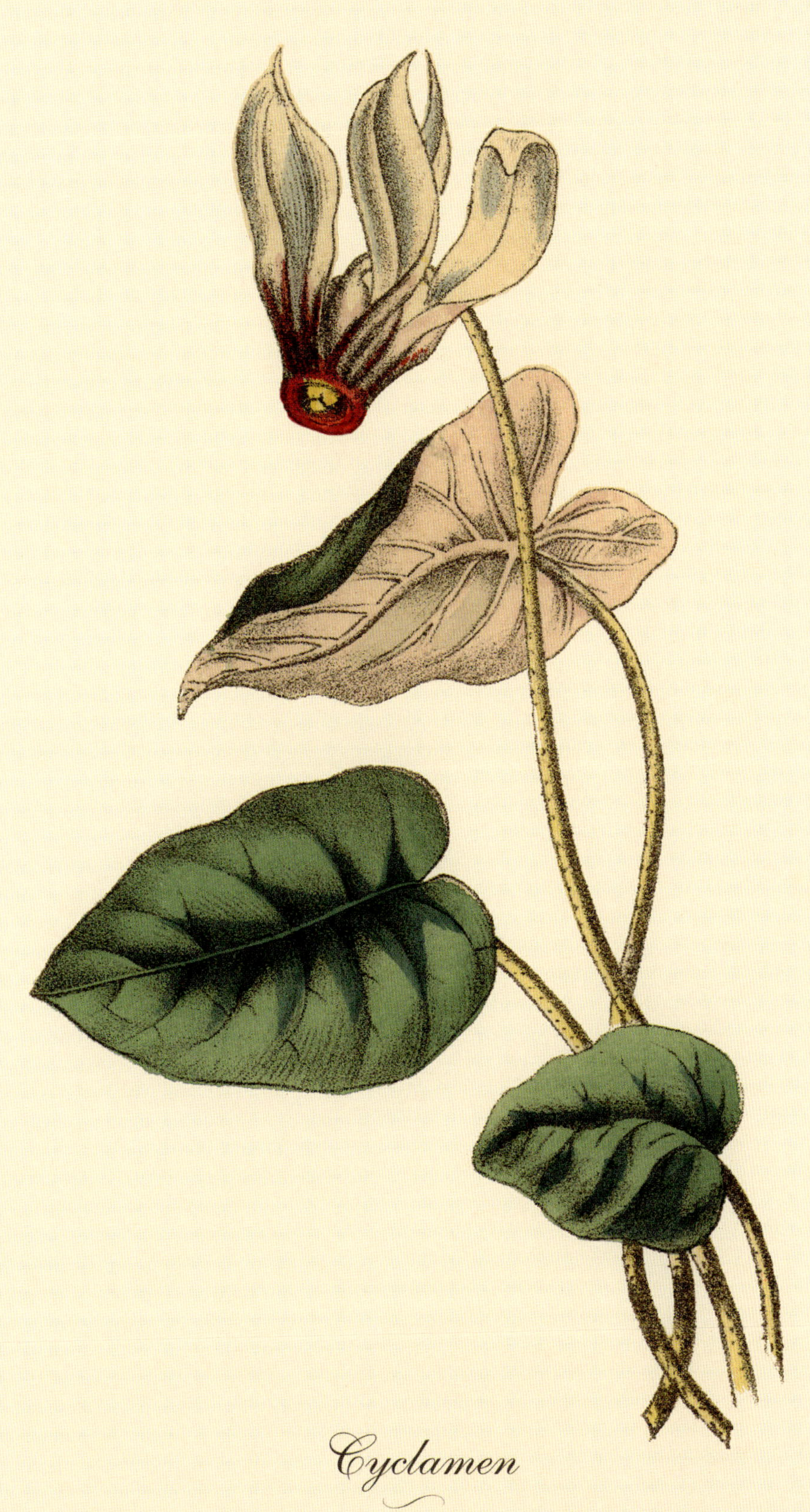

Cyclamen

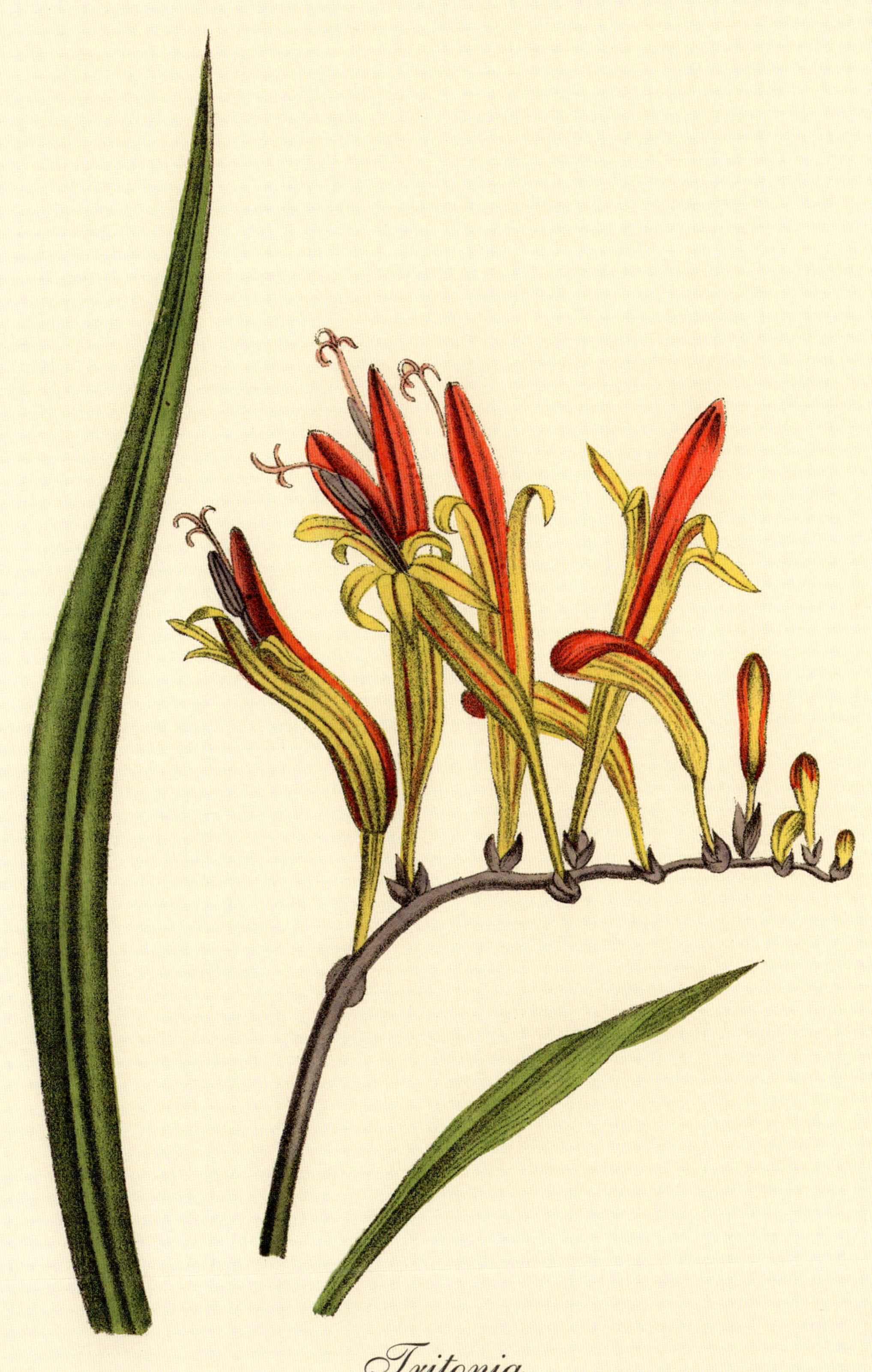

Tritonia

FLAME FREESIA

Illustration © Getty Images/bauhaus1000

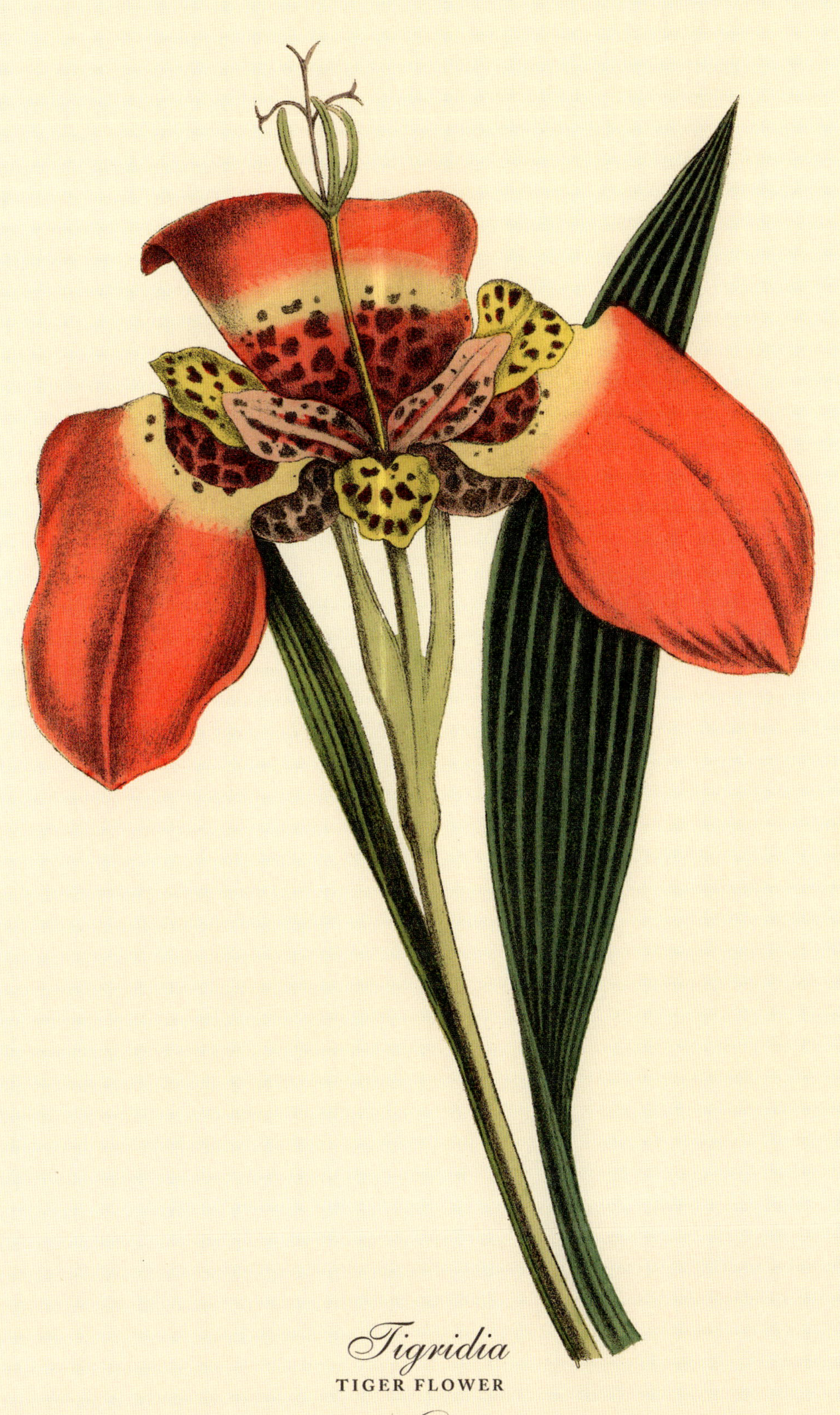

Tigridia

TIGER FLOWER

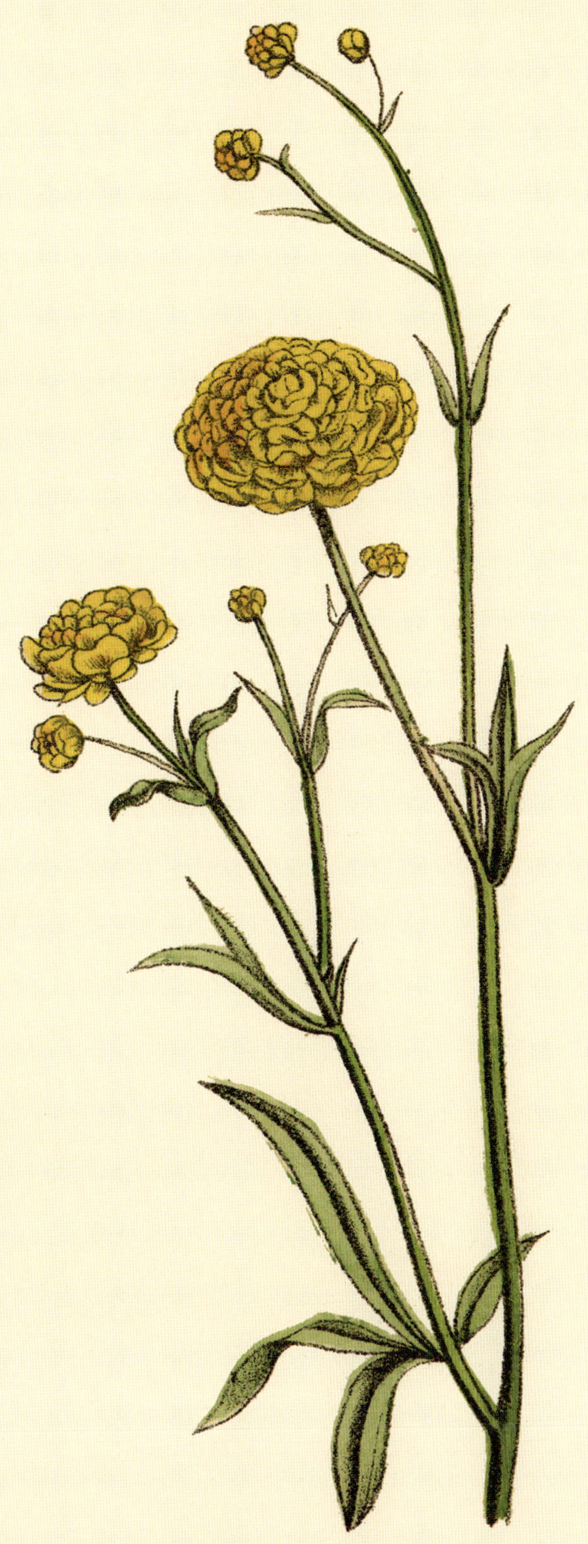

Ranunculus
BUTTERCUP

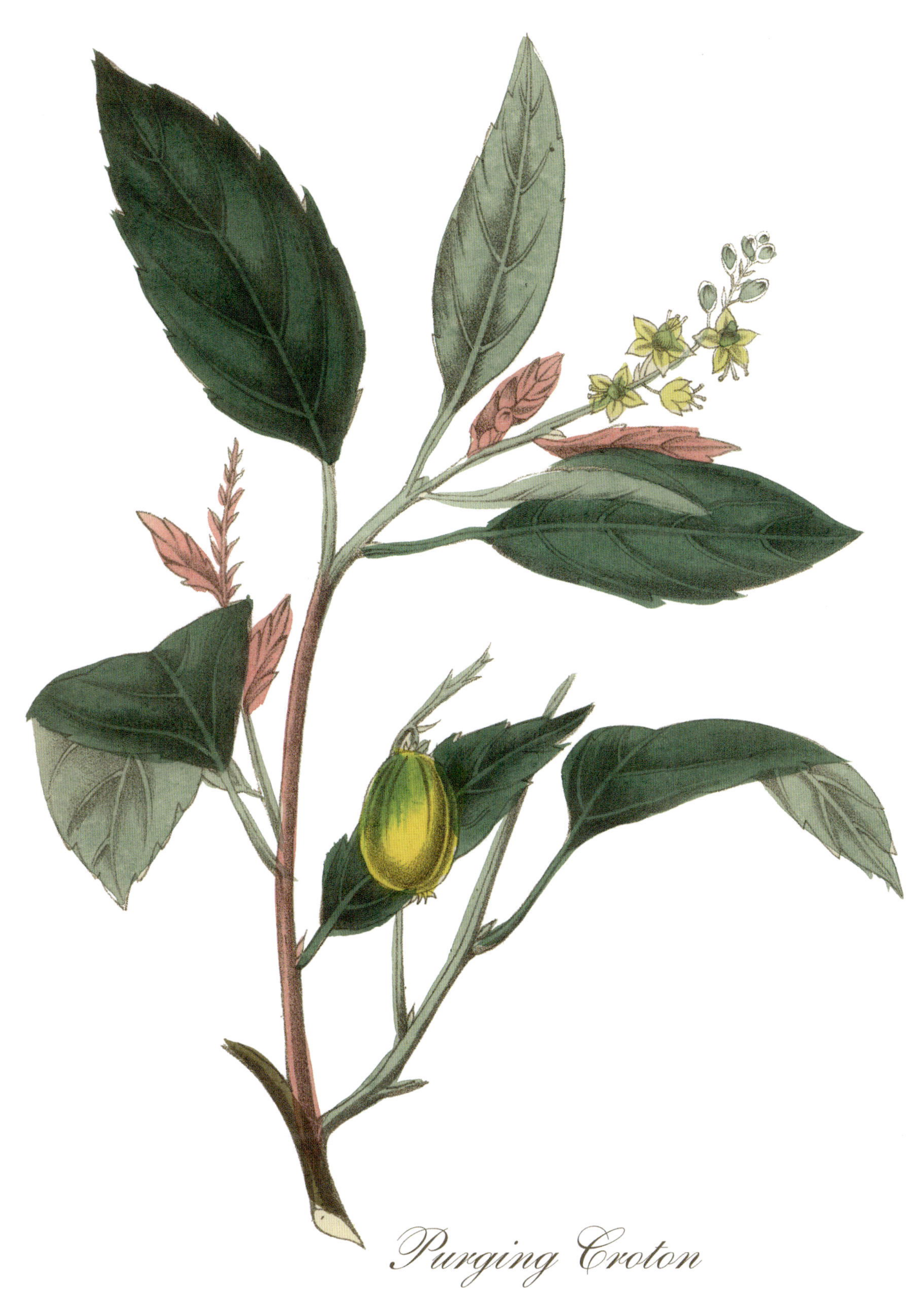

Purging Croton

Illustration © Getty Images/bauhaus1000

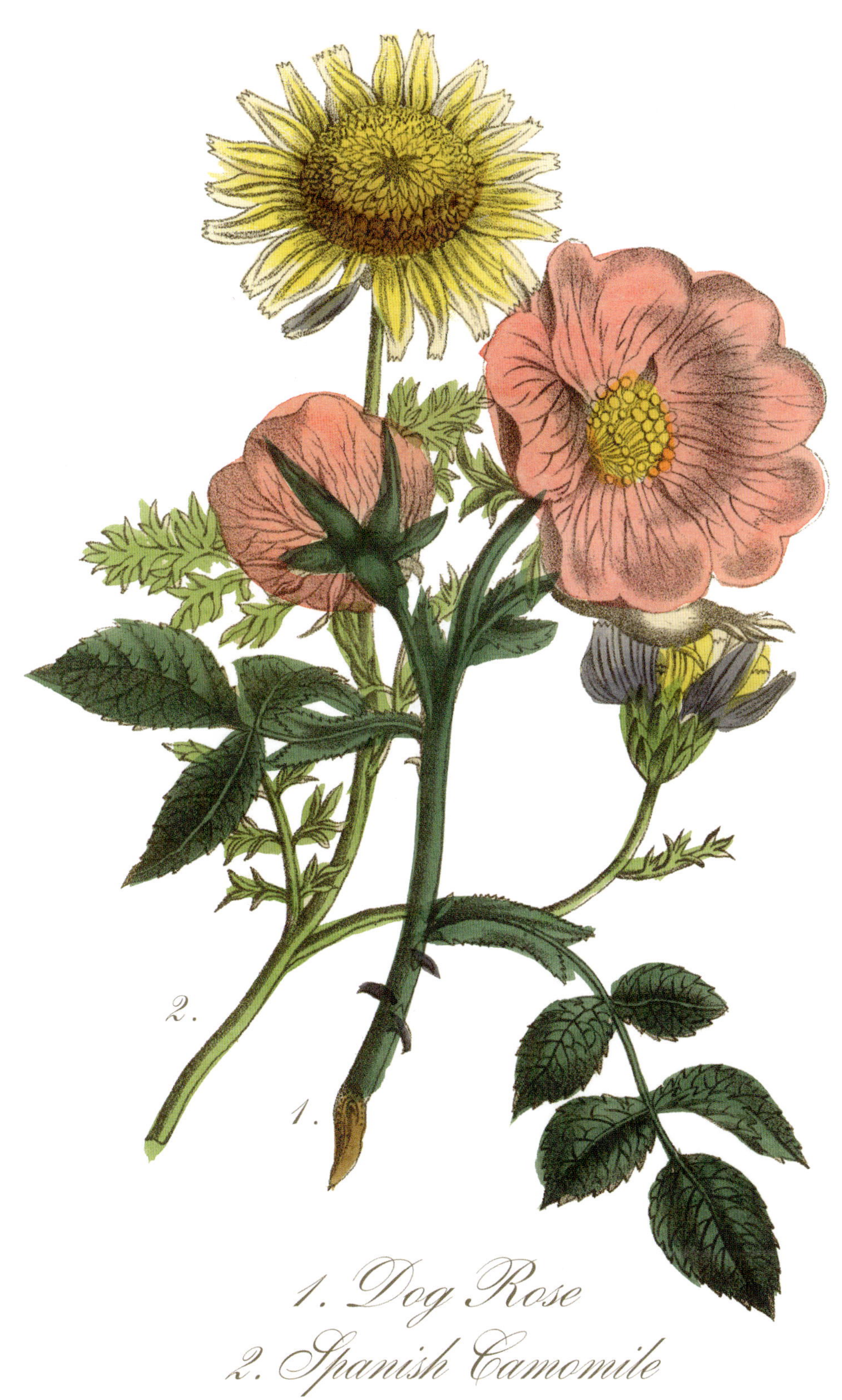

1. *Dog Rose*
2. *Spanish Camomile*

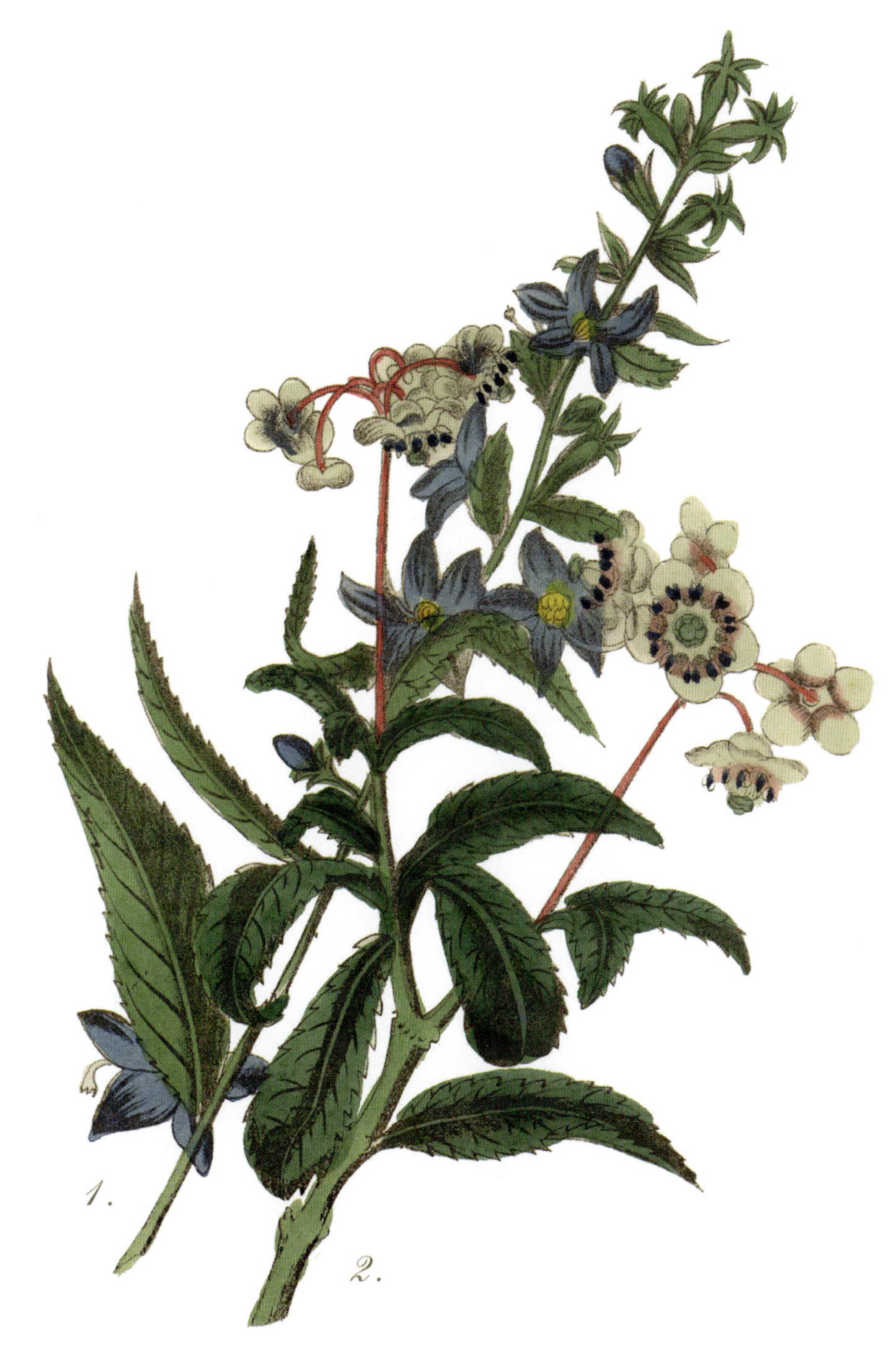

1. Blue Lobelia
2. Pipsissewa

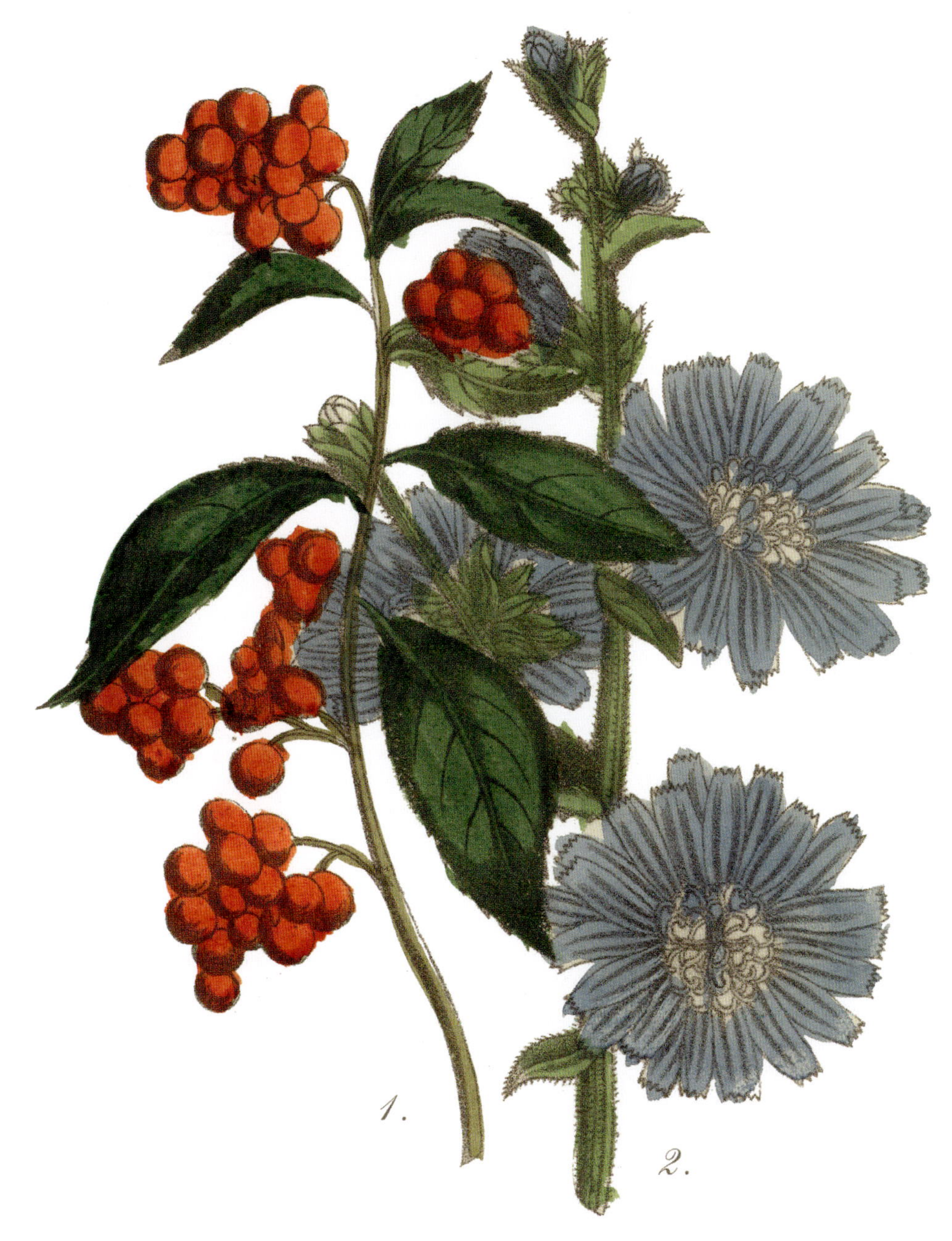

1. Bittersweet

2. Wild or Blue Succory

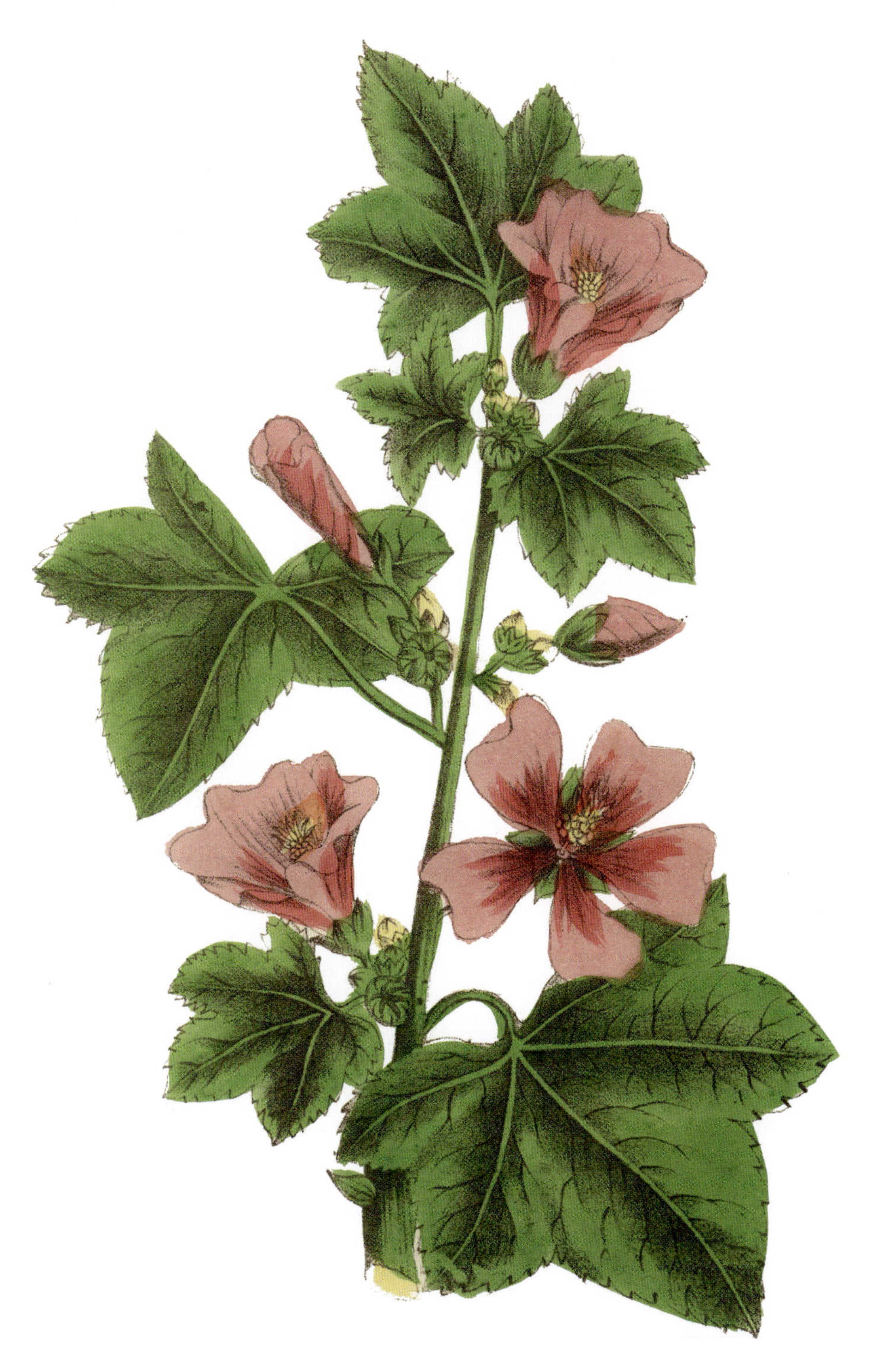

Common Mallow

Illustration © Getty Images/bauhaus1000

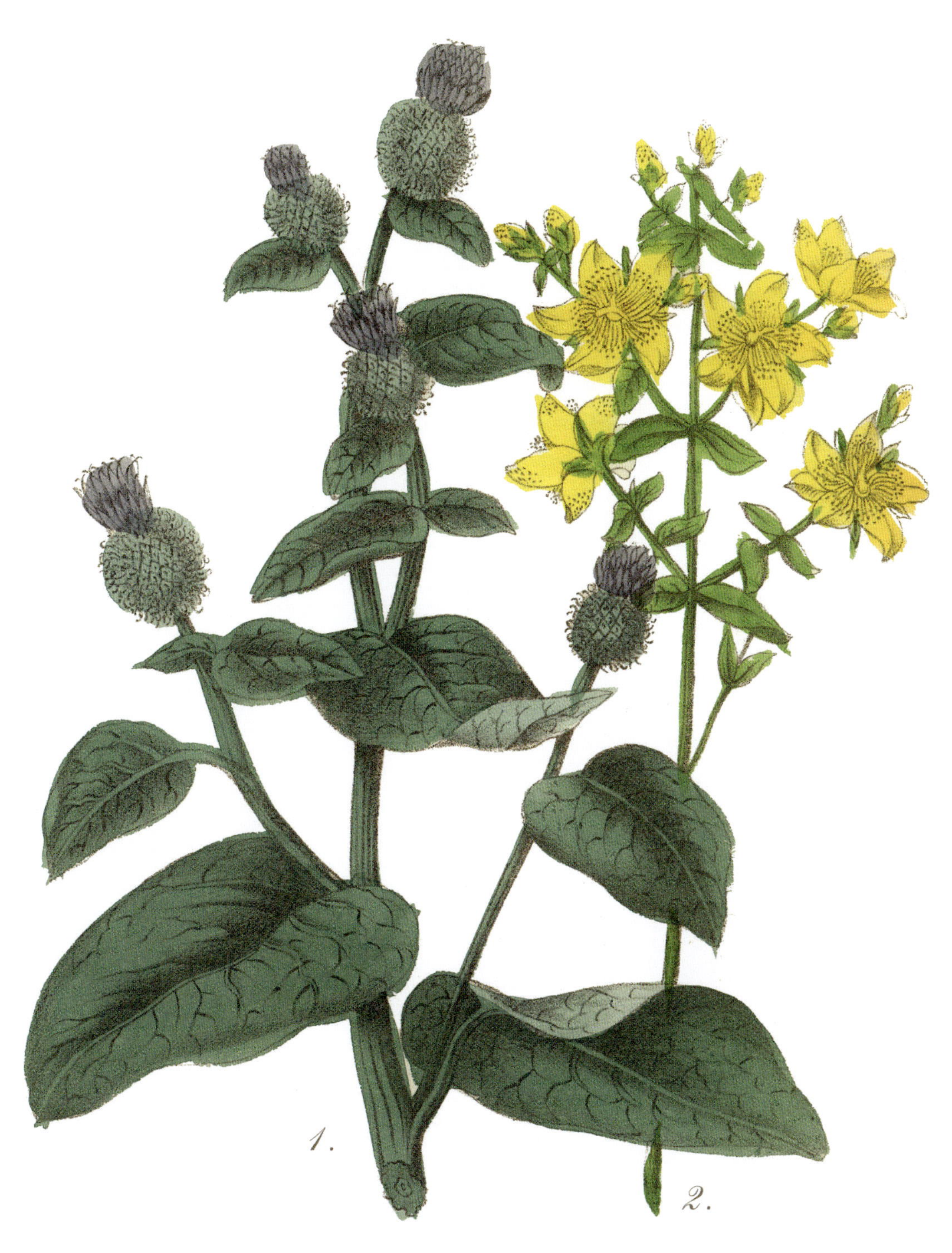

1. Burdock. 2. St. John's Wort.

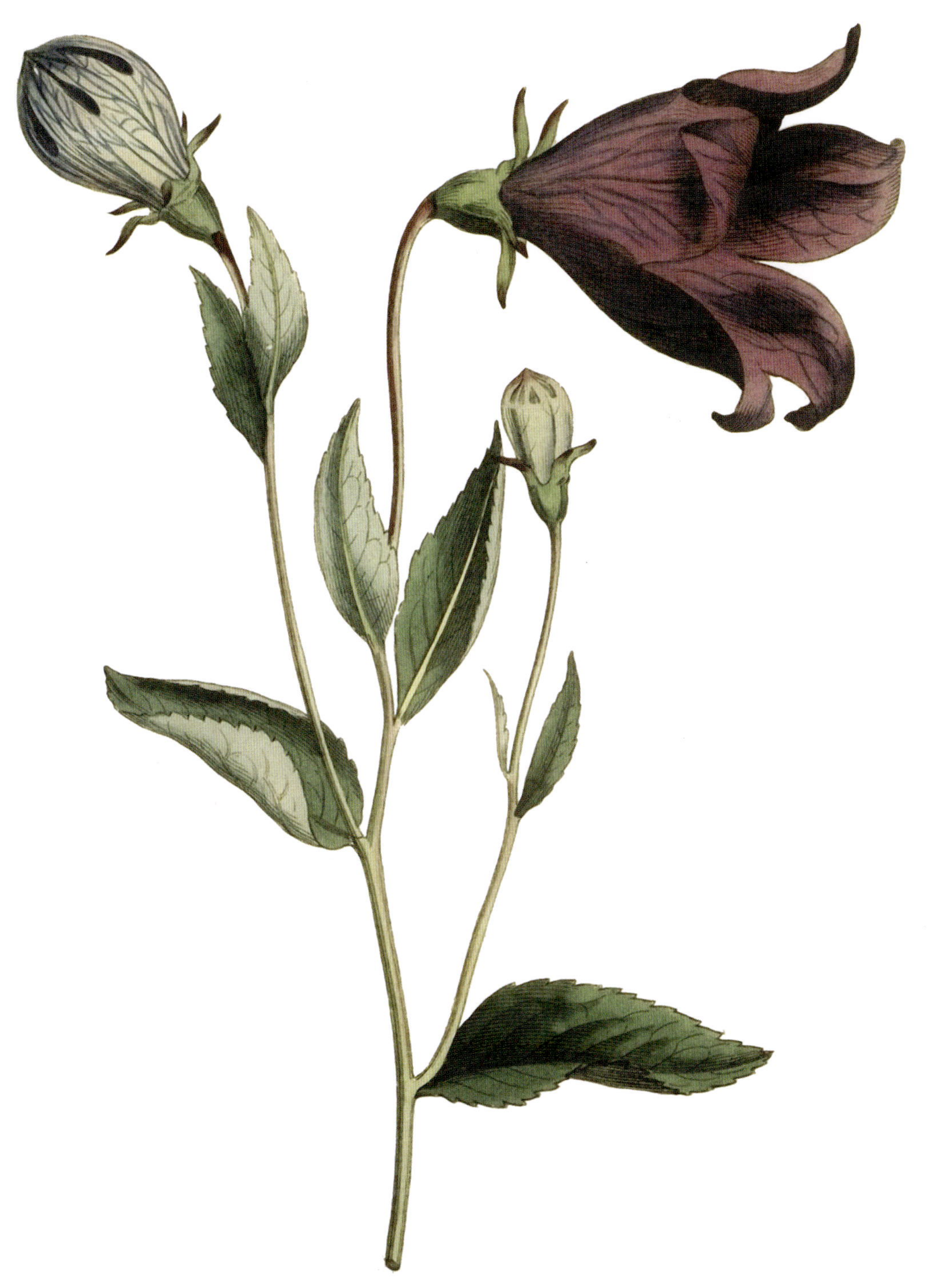

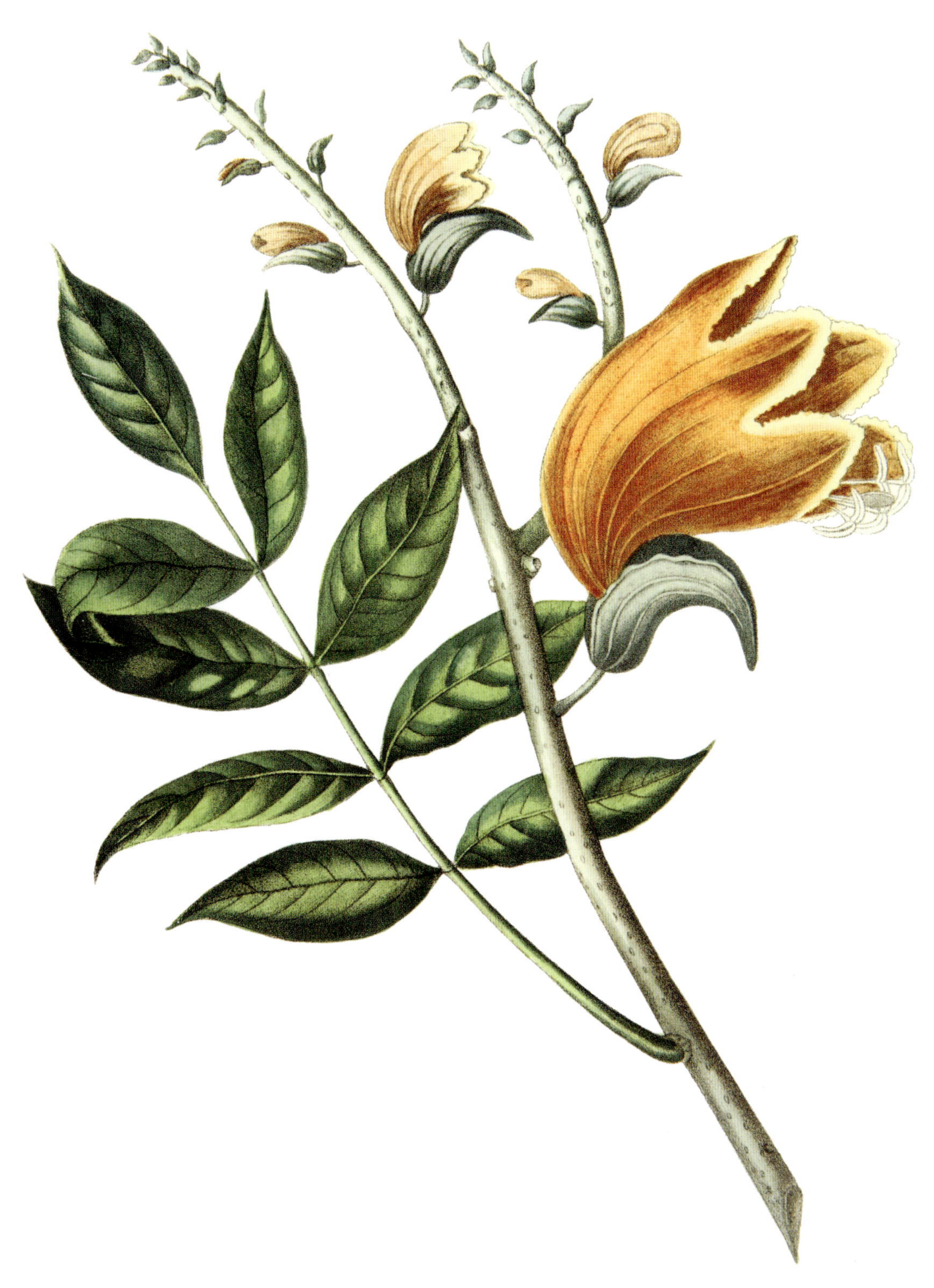

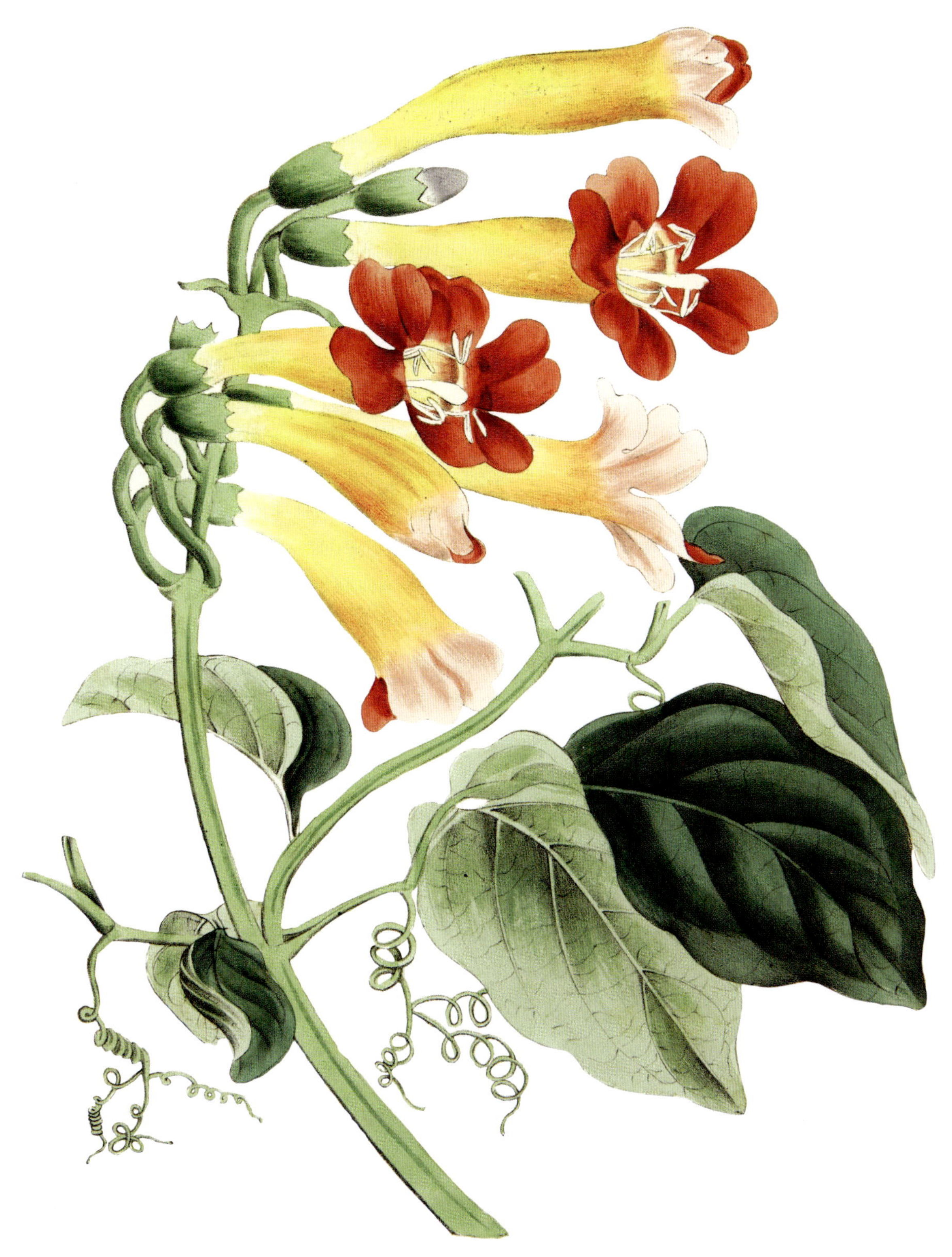

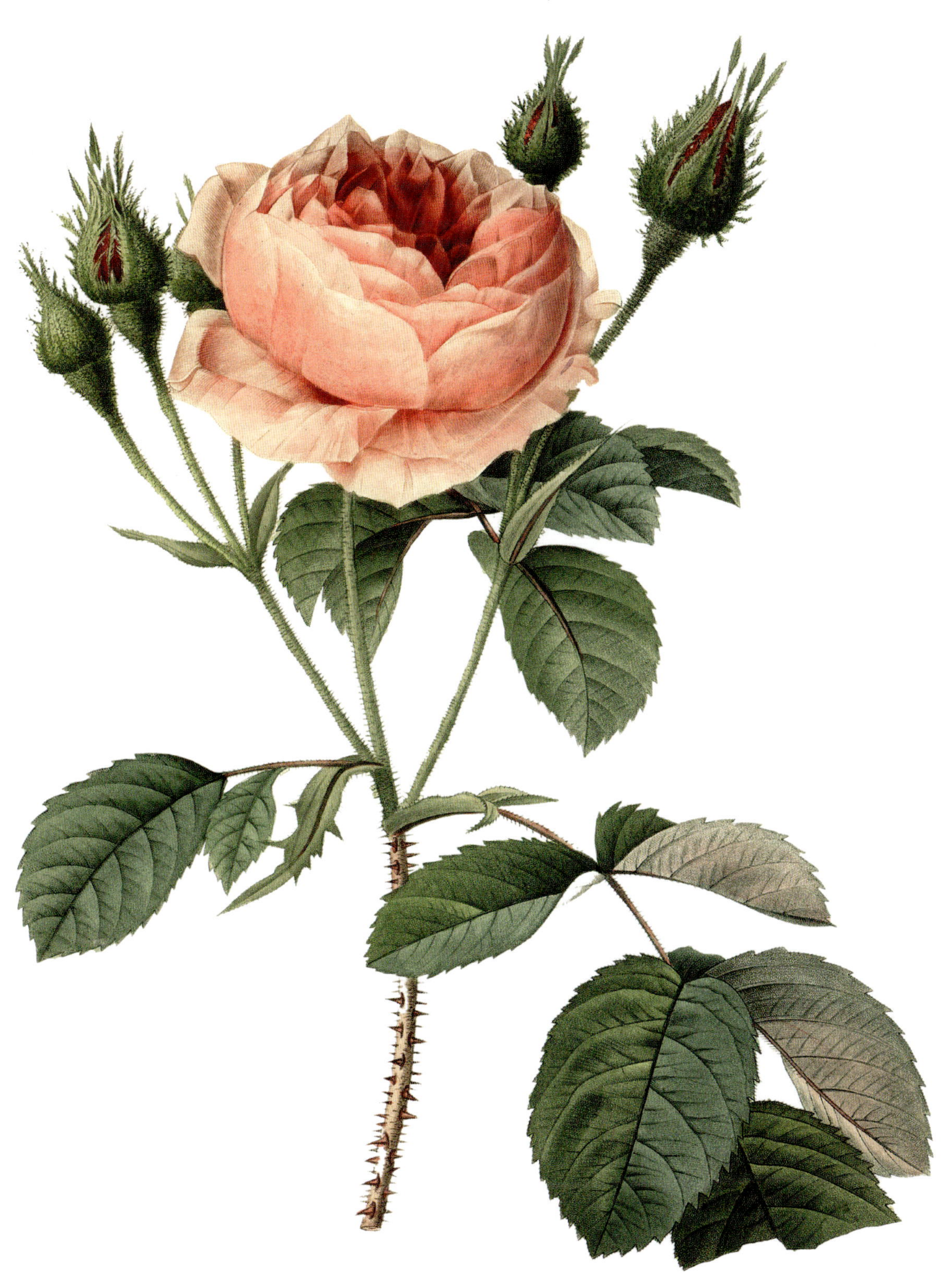

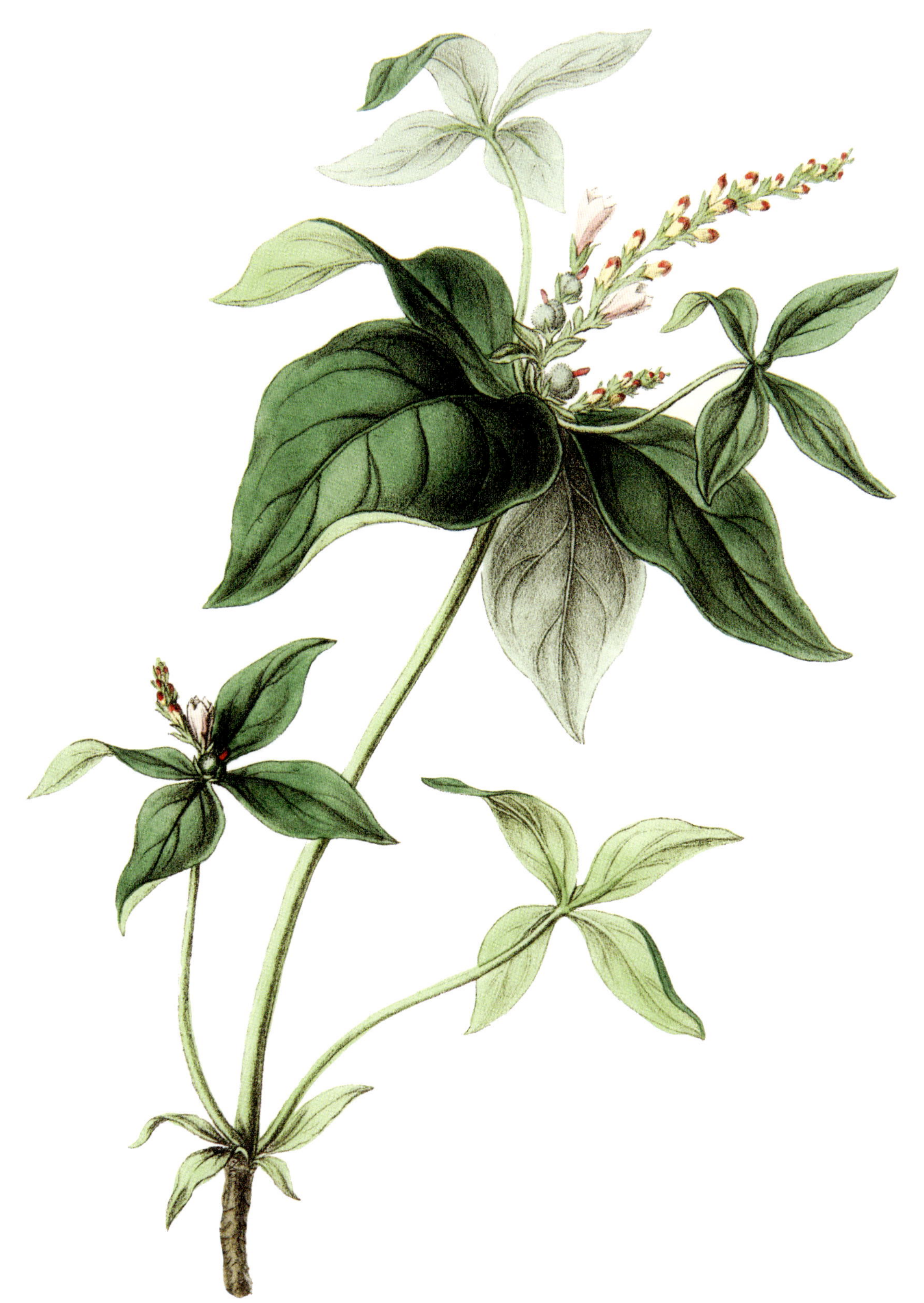

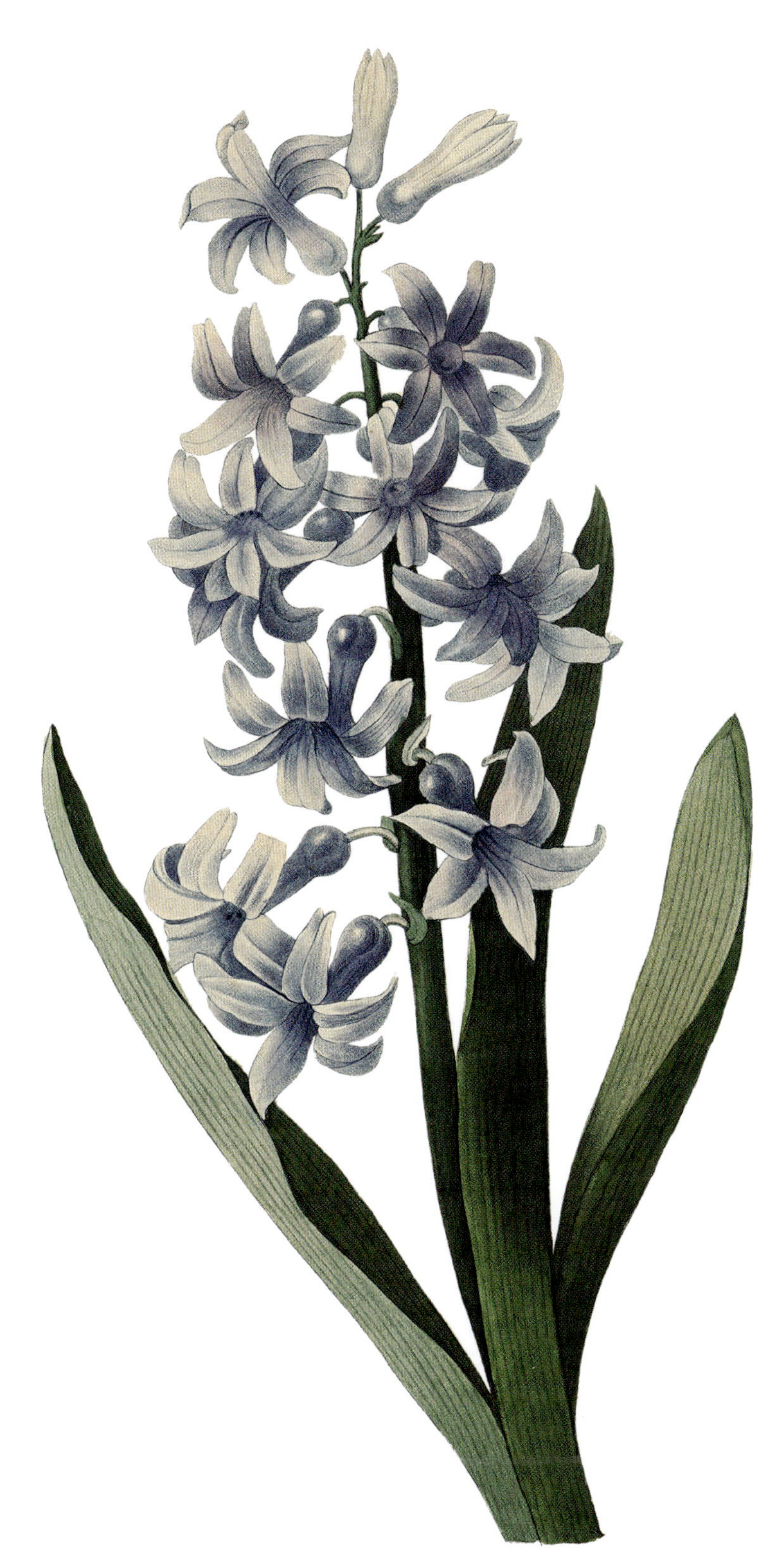

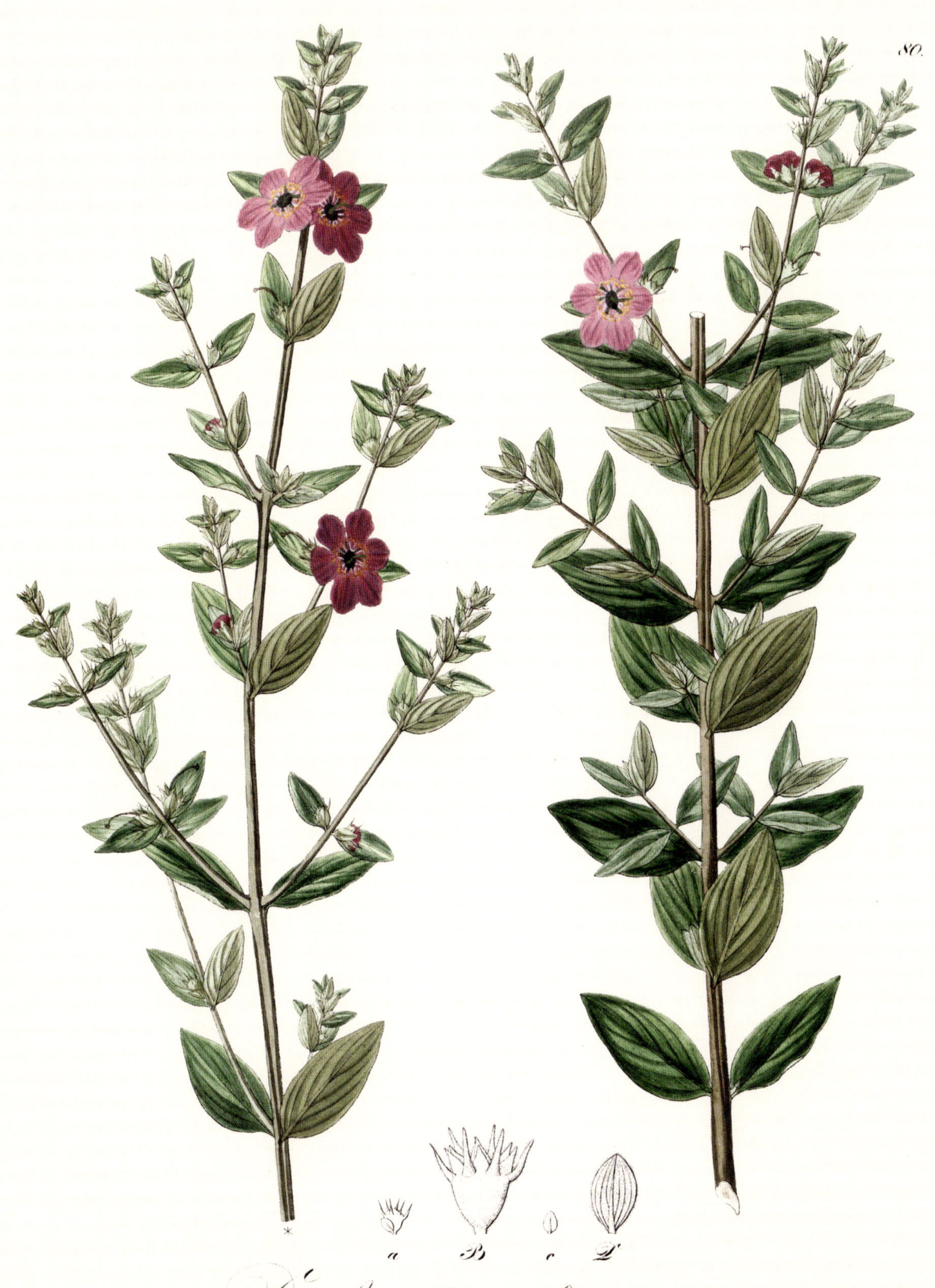

Diplusodon alutaceus.

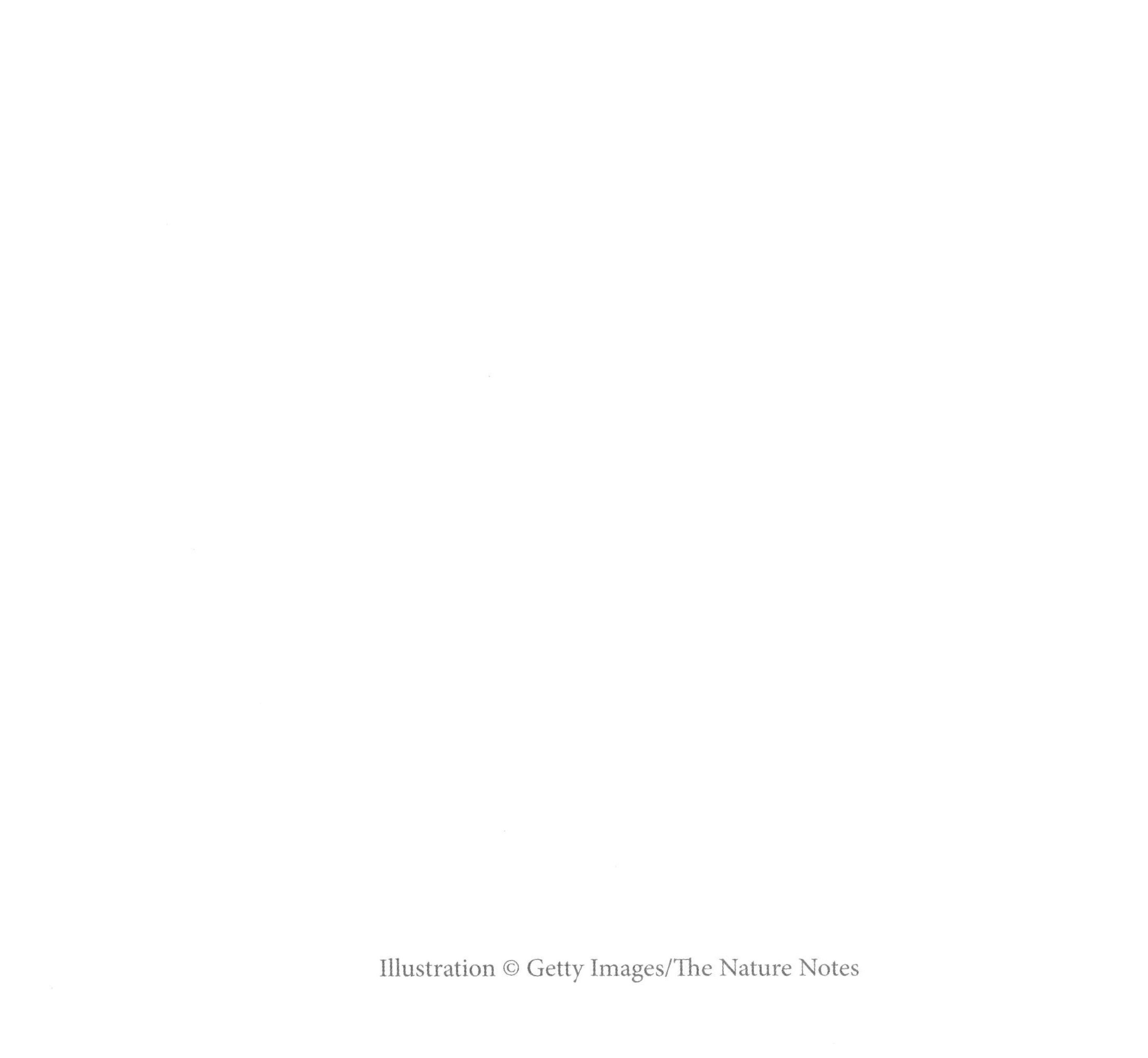

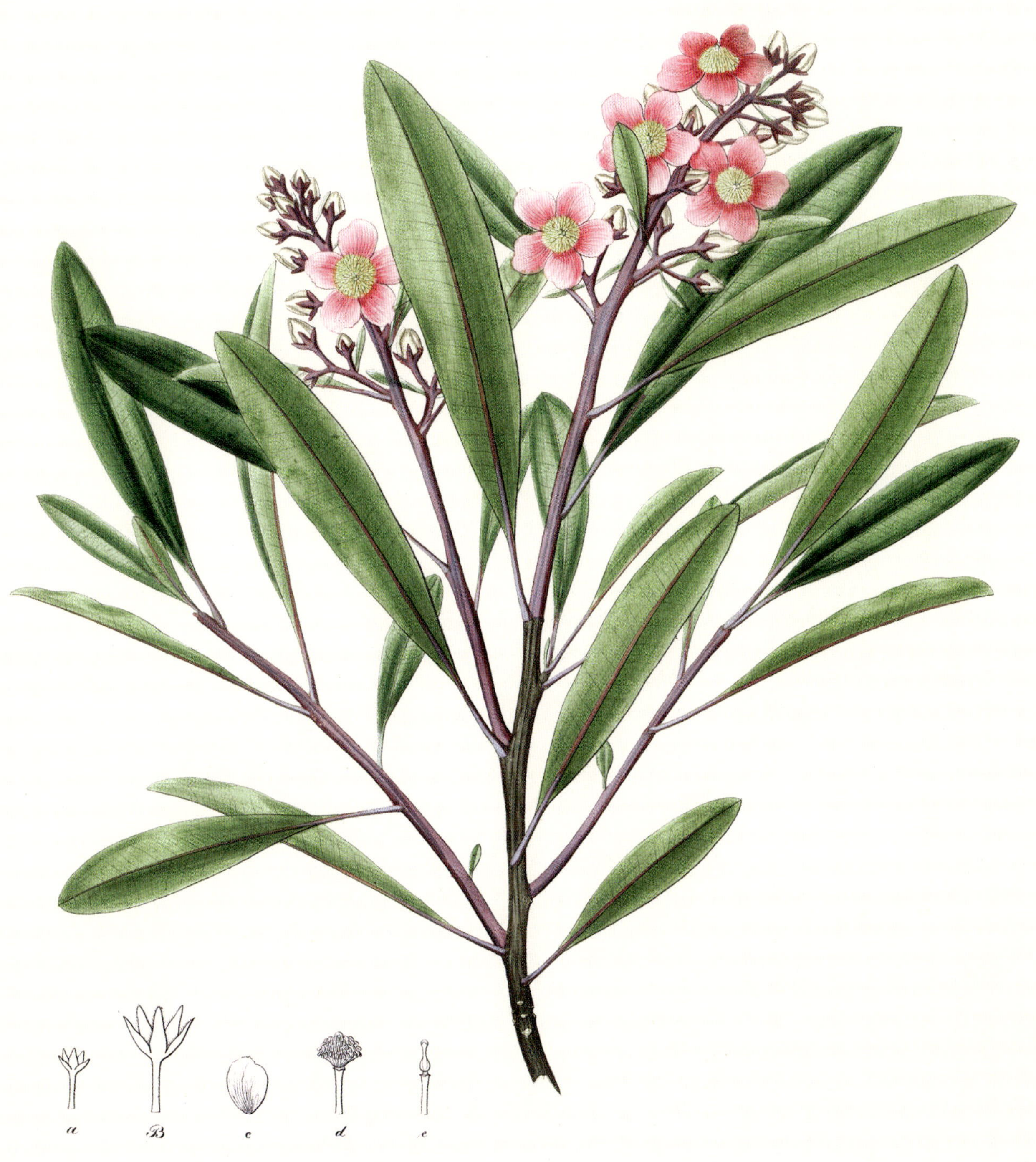

Kielmeyera angustifolia.

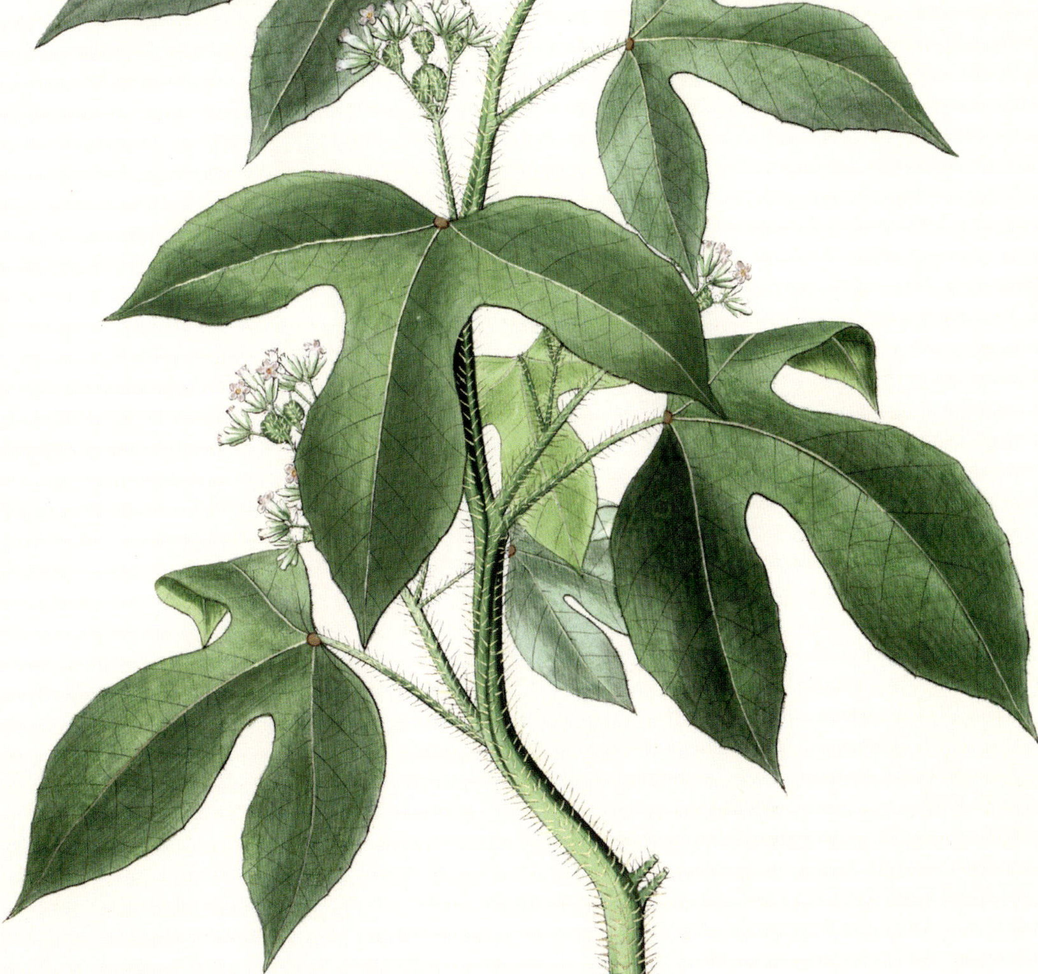

Cnidoscolus neglectus.

Sandler ad herb. delin et in lapid: exaravit.

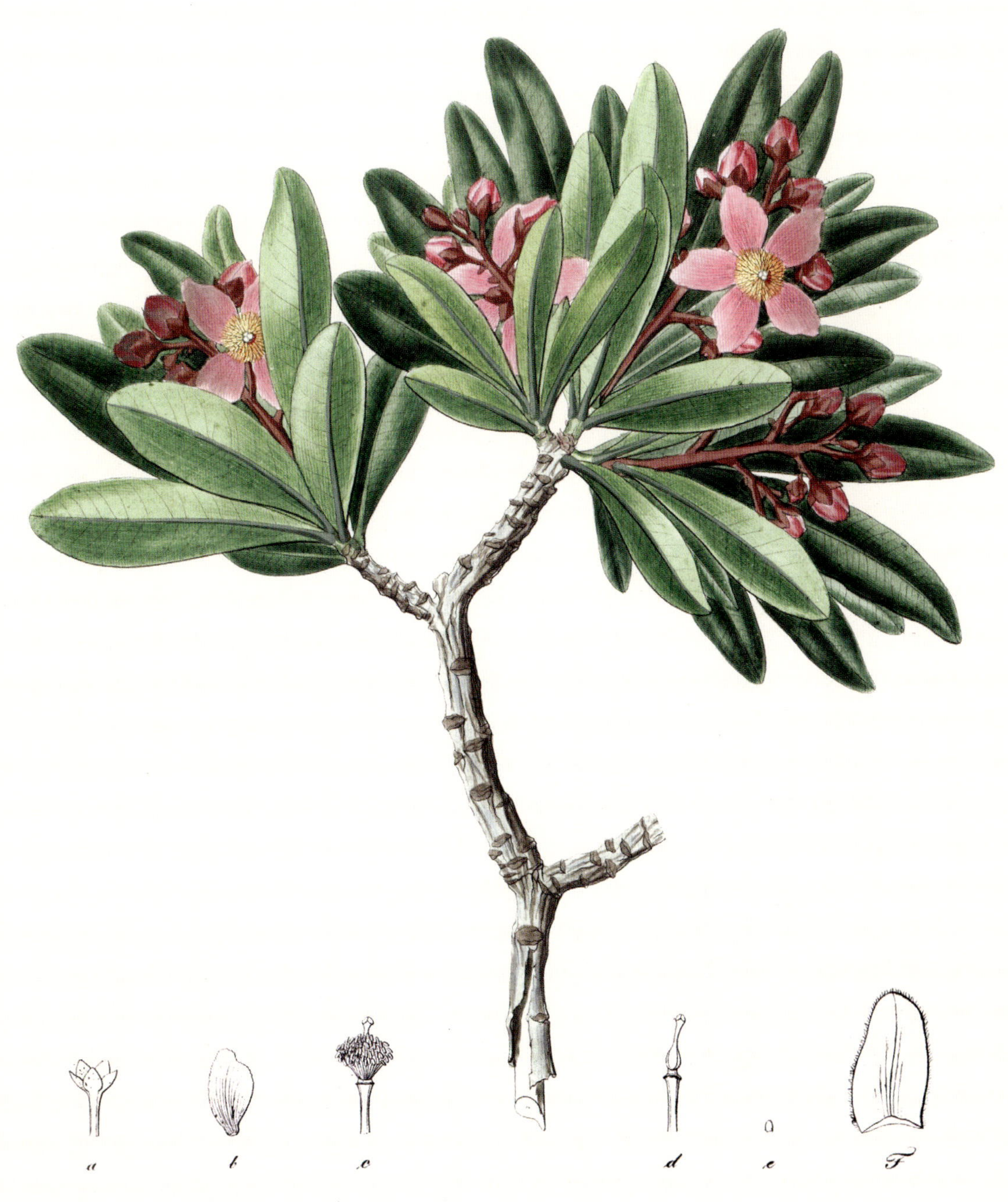

Kielmeyera microphylla.

83.

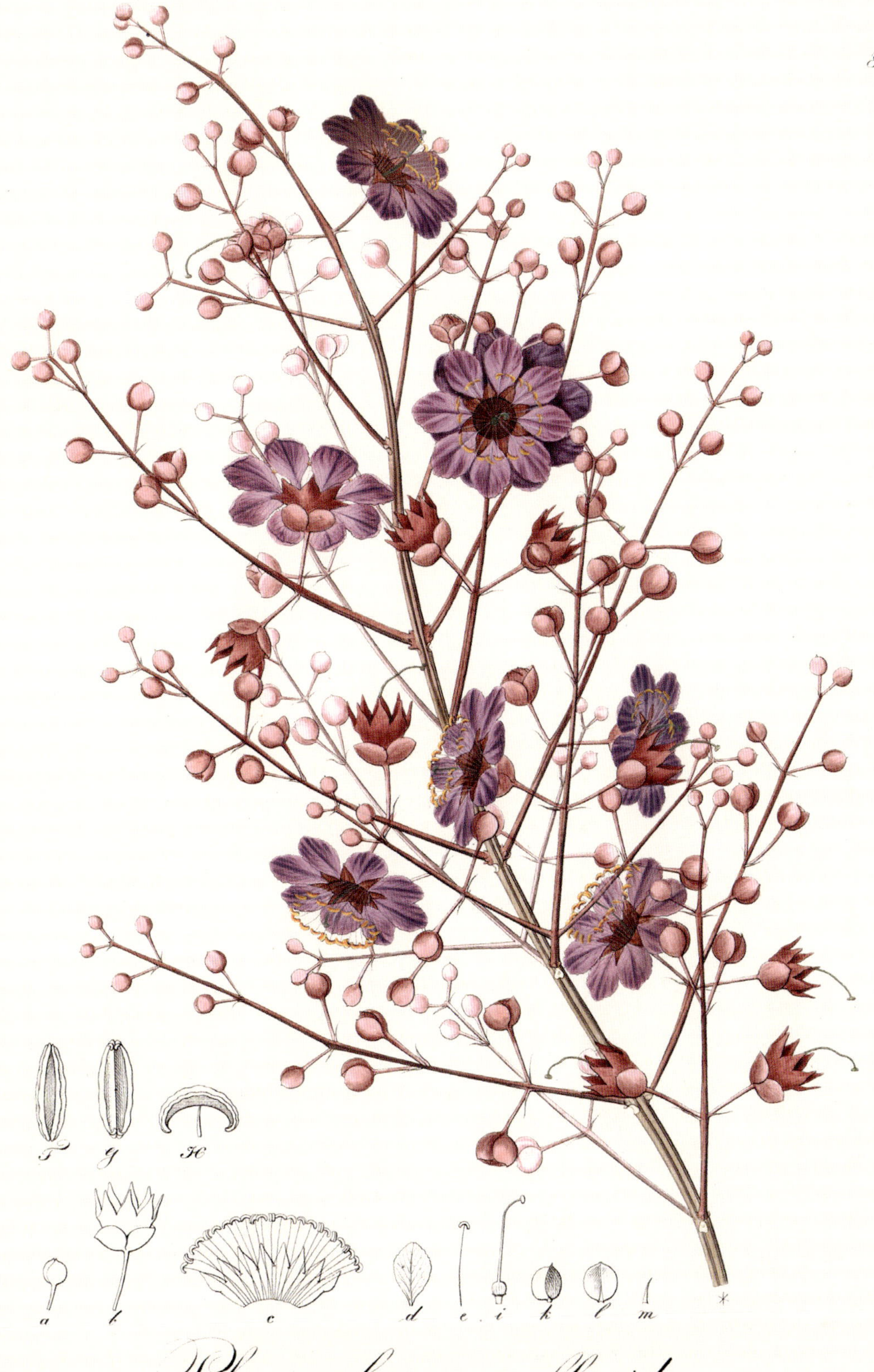

Physocalymma florida.

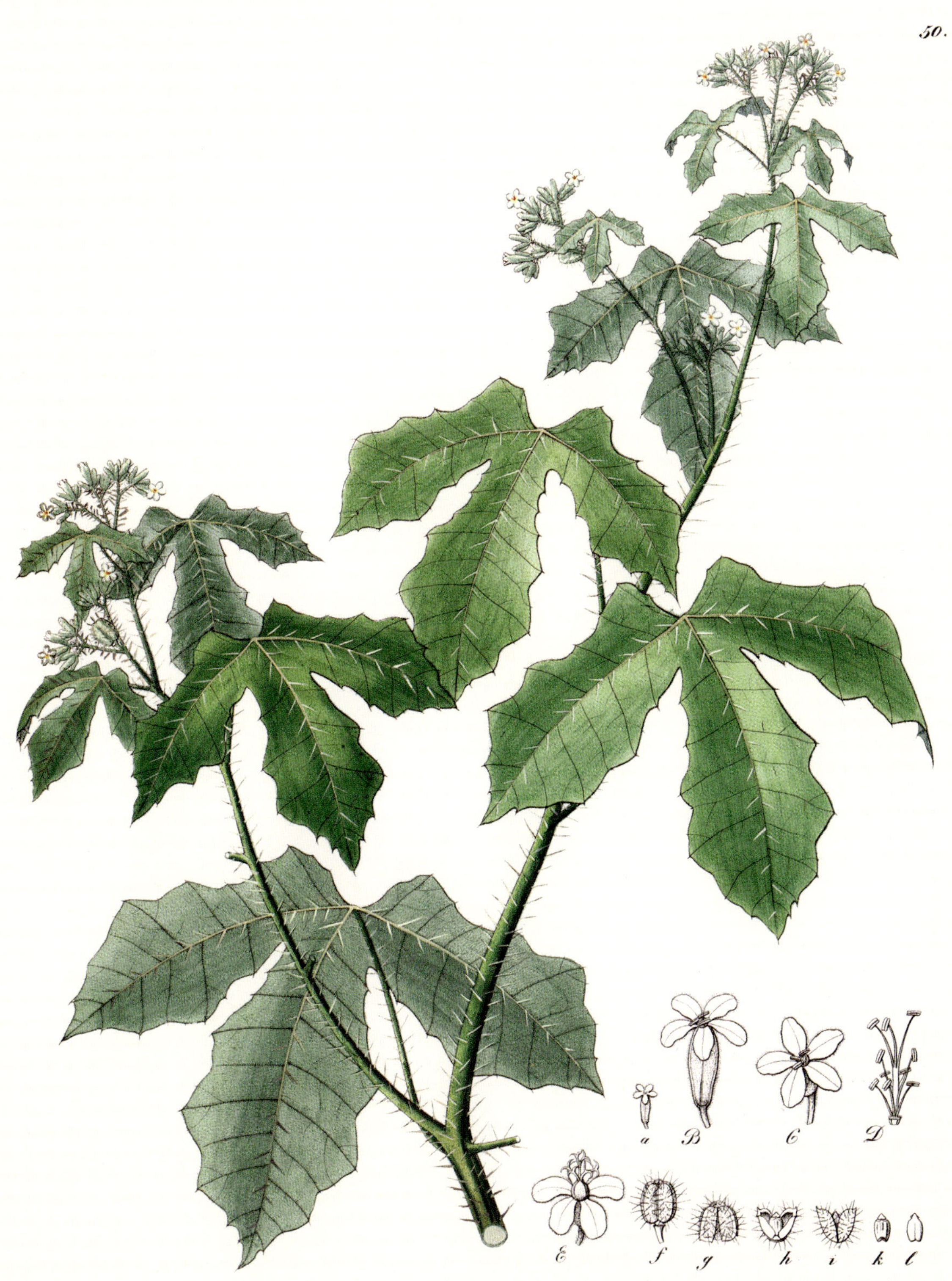

Cnidoscolus Marcgravii.

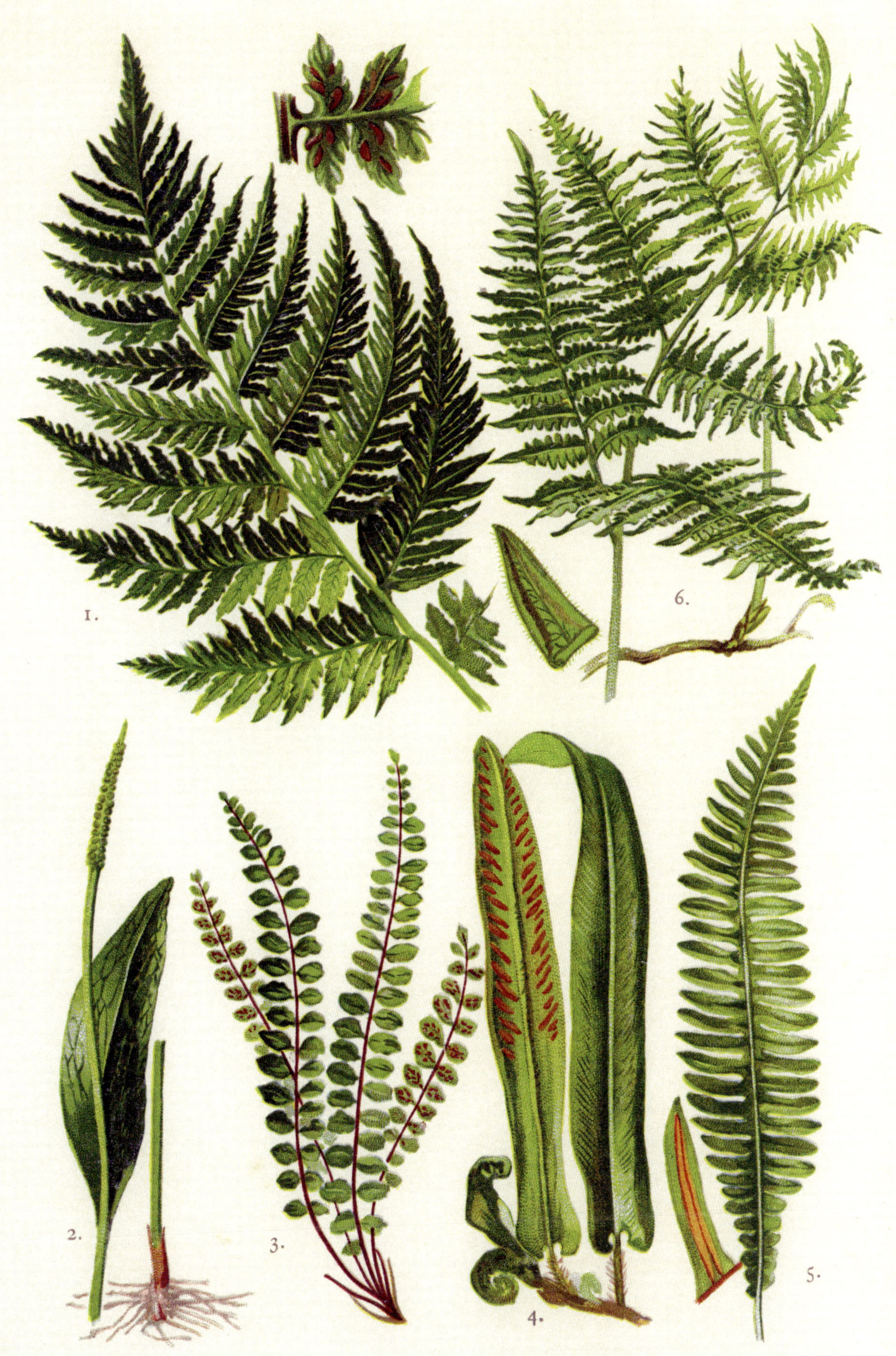

1.
6.
2.
3.
4.
5.